THE STORY TELLER

PROMISES

THE STORY TELLER

PROMISES

A Gallery of Biblical Portraits

Steve Stephens

PROMISE
PRESS
An Imprint of Barbour Publishing

© 2000 by Steve Stephens

ISBN 1-57748-851-2

Cover illustration: Lookout Design Group
                   www.lookoutdesign.com

Published by Promise Press, an imprint of Barbour Publishing, Inc., P.O. Box 719, Uhrichsville, Ohio 44683, http://www.barbourbooks.com

Member of the
Evangelical Christian
Publishers Association

Printed in the United States of America.

DEDICATION

To all who follow. . .
the purity of Light-Maker,
the peace of Comfort-Giver,
the joy of Heart-Lifter.

ACKNOWLEDGMENTS

The author gratefully acknowledges those whose lives and support have been integral to retelling these stories of Light-Maker, Comfort-Giver, and Heart-Lifter:

- Tami, my wonderful wife, for being patient and supportive and encouraging.

- Sue and Linda, for typing tirelessly and without complaint.

- Paul Ingram, for valuable input and insightful editing.

- Susan Schlabach and everyone at Promise Press, for believing in this project.

- All the wonderful people at KPDQ and True Talk 800 AM, for the opportunity to stretch and grow in an entirely new arena.

- The caring church community at MFBC, for constantly pointing to the one beyond the sky in both words and deeds.

- The Sunday night group, for their vision and push to live life the way it was meant to be lived.

- All my family (children, parents, brothers, sisters, nieces, nephews, uncles, aunts, in-laws), for always being close.

INTRODUCTION

Endings can be the best.

It's the getting there that can be difficult.

The prophets of the Old Testament did not see the end. They stood under a sky where all the stars had set, but there was not yet a hint of light on the eastern horizon. Very little light shone down on the people. Those who represented the one beyond the sky had to speak of despair and destruction. Yet they also spoke of marvelous Hope. In the midst of collapsing kingdoms and prolonged captivity, wonderful promises were given.

Hope comes in many shapes in this book. Here we can take a fresh look at some of the best-known and most-loved stories in all of the Bible—

Jonah and the big fish;

Daniel in the lions' den;

Esther, the Jewish girl who became queen of Persia.

Hope is powerful in the very different love story of Hosea and Gomer. Hope flickered but burned in the lives of Hosea's prophetic colleagues, Ezekiel and Jeremiah. A nation was reborn of Hope under Ezra the priest and Nehemiah the administrator. Hope survived tyranny under the sheer courage and determination of the Maccabees. Mingled with these giants of faith are a host of lesser known but highly significant kings and priests and scoundrels. Some of these knew Hope. They also knew the consequences of rebellious desires and unworthy goals and spiritual failure.

With the three previous books in the Story Teller Series—*Beginnings, Leaders,* and *Kingdoms*—this volume distills parts of thirty-two Old Testament books into 120 stories. First Maccabees is added to tell a bit about events that came after the close of the Hebrew canon. Its historical narrative is recognized by biblical scholars as both accurate and valuable.

These four volumes present the Scriptures of Judaism and Christianity in a lively style that straddles boundaries of poetic metaphor and historical narrative and dramatic realism. Like the timeless narratives on which they are based, these stories are not simply about people or events. They seek to discover the one who is infinite and eternal and all-powerful through eleven descriptive names:

1. Garden-Maker
2. Promise-Keeper
3. Bondage-Breaker
4. Land-Giver
5. People-Builder
6. King-Maker
7. Hope-Giver
8. Truth-Holder
9. Light-Maker
10. Comfort-Giver
11. Heart-Lifter

Through these names, a little insight is perhaps revealed about the one who holds stars in his hands, the one of whom Shepherd-King sang some three millennia ago:

As the deer pants for water,
So I thirst for you.
As the deer climbs to the highlands,
So I long to walk with you.
As the deer lies down to rest,
So I close my tired eyes
    and know that you are all I ever need.
                    —based on Psalm 18:33; 42:1–2; 62:1–7

PART 1
THE LIGHT-MAKER

TABLE OF CONTENTS
THE LIGHT-MAKER

Prologue 15

1. The Prosperous King (2 Kings 14:23–29; Jonah 1:1–3) 17

2. The Reluctant Prophet (Jonah) 22

3. The Farmer (Amos) 28

4. The Faithless Wife (Hosea) 33

5. The Decline (2 Kings 15:8–22) 40

6. The Invasion (2 Kings 15:23–29) 45

7. The Collapse (2 Kings 15:30; 17) 51

Epilogue 56

PROLOGUE

Tears rode the wrinkles of the old man's weathered face.

The fire crackled and blazed, its flames stretching toward the sky. The small circle watched the ancient storyteller as he stood silently in his plain white robe. His tears glistened in the red and orange hues of the firelight.

"Why do you cry?" asked the girl-child who had not yet finished her ninth year.

"I have read again the words of the Farmer and the Shopkeeper," said the old man. "Such sorrow."

"But why would the one beyond the sky allow such sorrow?" she asked.

"A big question for such a little one," the old man said with a laugh. "I have lived many times your years, and I have only a very small part of the answer as to why he uses such deep sorrow to do wonderful things. He uses it to give us a new name and a bright promise and a deeper faith."

"I don't understand."

"Watch," he said. The storyteller produced a small leather pouch from the folds of his robe. He carefully shook out a generous mound of powder into his cupped hand and put the pouch away. Then, with a sudden expansive movement, he cast the powder into the midst of the flame.

WHOOSH! It seemed as if the fire had been sucked right out of the wood that had blazed so merrily. Neither moon nor stars shone through the clouds. The world was a very dark place, so dark that the little girl could not tell whether her eyes were open or closed, so dark that children whimpered, and even adults felt uneasy.

But then everyone could see the tiny glow that moved back and forth. It was the old man's walking stick, which he had placed next to the fire. Its tip glowed with a tiny burning ember. How bright it seemed. His voice sang out.

"No matter how dark the night seems, the one who holds the stars in his hands is the maker of light. He does not always take away sorrows. But he always shines through them."

Was it their imagination? The sky had been so dark. Now a break in the clouds blew by the moon. Its crescent gleamed. The old man stirred his walking stick through the embers, and the flames burst up once more.

"I have given you a new name for the one who is above all. He is Light-Maker, and the sacred scroll shall reveal what that name means."

Everyone leaned forward, and the fire pushed back the darkness.

IT IS USUALLY
THE FIERCEST ENEMY
WHOSE NEED CRIES OUT
FOR THE DEEPEST COMPASSION.

CHAPTER 1

THE PROSPEROUS KING

In the beginning of the Blue Planet there was a garden. It was an amazing place of beauty and wonder and perfection. It was a paradise of peace, bounded by the four rivers.

A seedbed for delicate roses and stately oaks.

A meadow where deer grazed fearlessly.

A home with lions slumbering harmlessly in the sun.

To the south was the Great River that would one day carry ships to the City of the Moon, where Merchant would learn the name of Promise-Keeper. To the north was the Golden River. The two rivers were twins and between their sparkling waters Man met Woman.

Man and Woman loved the garden, and they loved Garden-Maker, but when Shining One offered them the choice, they did not choose wisely. So Shining One raised a barrier between the people, touching every heart with pride and pain and anarchy. He clouded the eyes of the man and the woman, so they could scarcely see the Garden-Maker.

But Garden-Maker himself set a barrier between the first couple and the garden. An angel of terrible light barred the way to their beautiful land forever, swinging his sword of flame back and forth, to and fro.

After many summers, the descendants of the man and the woman turned the entire Blue Planet into a place of violence fashioned after the ways of Shining One. So utterly had they turned from the maker of the garden that he washed them all from the soil of the Blue Planet, cleansing it of its poisons. One man, Builder, had not forgotten the garden or its maker.

He learned to walk by his side each morning before the sun touched the Mountains of the Dawn. So Garden-Maker remade the surface of the Blue Planet, planting Builder and his family to blossom there.

After many more summers, the great-grandson of Builder roamed restlessly upon the Blue Planet. His name was Hunter, and it was he who wanted to touch the sky, so he built a great ziggurat and called it the Gateway to Heaven. But Shining One was its principle architect, and therefore the one beyond the sky reached down and unmade it. Hunter never reached the sky, but he built more cities. One was the City of Blood on the Golden River. Another was the City of Stars on the Great River. Around both cities grew great kingdoms with mighty kings. The cities became twin kingdoms on twin rivers.

They shared a common language.

They built a common way of life.

They felt a common love for Shining One.

The Kingdom of the Bull and the Kingdom of the Dragon were filled with the hatred and the darkness and the anarchy of Shining One. They fought for dominance over the centuries. For a time, the bull was the strongest and then the dragon grew stronger, then the bull was once again in control.

It was when the Bull raged in power that a king watched the two closely from across the fertile crescent, toward the Great Sea. The son of Strong King was the fourth in the line of the Sword Dynasty and knew no fear of any nation. Many years before, his kingdom had been ruled by Wise King. It had been a time of peace and glory; this king was sure he could regain the wonder of that time. His was the Northern Kingdom. It was no longer so large and prosperous as in the days of Wise King. But his hand felt strong, and he was sure that his would be a new golden time. All that was really needed was to make the City of Caravans his own. With that great empire of wealth, he would move alongside the Kingdom of the Bull. It would be a hard undertaking, so he went to see a respected elder of the people, a man who was tall and balding and ruddy of complexion.

"What shall I do?" asked the king.

"That is a most important question," said the older man. Since his youth he had served the great Seer. Now his master had left the Blue Planet, and this Reluctant Prophet was the new truth teller to the northern kings. "If I tell you," said the prophet, "will you do it?"

"I will do whatever makes my kingdom great once more."

"Then look beyond the sky and you will see the maker of light," said the tall, balding man. "Many summers ago, Wise King declared to his people that 'Light is better than darkness.' It was this truth, more than his great wealth and lands and military conquests, that made the kingdom great. The words are still true, and that greatness is within your reach."

"Yes, yes; I've heard all that before," said the king with an impatient wave of his hand. "But if I go north with my army against the City of Caravans, will I be successful?"

"If you follow the ways of Light-Maker, you shall prosper and stretch the boundaries of your kingdom."

"Who is Light-Maker?"

"The one above all has many names:

"First he was known as Garden-Maker.

"Merchant called him Promise-Keeper.

"General knew him as Bondage-Breaker;

"Your great-grandfather called him Truth-Holder.

"In this time you should call the one who holds stars in his hands, Light-Maker. He is the source of all light. If you turn your back on him, you will stumble through darkness until you fall."

"My great-grandfather followed Truth-Holder, but did he find greatness?" asked the king.

"When I anointed him Sword King some forty summers ago, he looked beyond the sky. He did much good in the beginning, but in the end he bowed to the golden calves."

"I want lasting greatness, so I will follow Light-Maker all the days of my life," said the king. "Never will I bow to the golden calves."

"Then the one above all will give you the land south of the City of Caravans and north of the Valley of Salt."

The king smiled, for he knew the Reluctant Prophet spoke only the truth. He ordered every man of fighting age to meet before the Ivory Palace at the next full moon. A mighty army gathered with sharpened swords and sturdy shields and well-oiled chariots drawn by fine-bred horses. Thousands of valiant warriors, ready for war, stood before the king of the Northern Kingdom.

"Without Light-Maker there can be no victory," shouted the king, "and with him there can be no defeat."

The warriors cheered until the very walls of the capital seemed to shake. The army marched from the gates north until it reached the City of Caravans. When the city fell, they marched south to the Valley of Salt. The boundaries had been stretched, just as the Reluctant Prophet had foretold.

With the Northern Kingdom strong and secure, the king's wealth grew. Such a time of peace and prosperity had not been seen since the days of Wise King. Gifts from throughout the known world were set before the Prosperous King.

Silver and gold,

silk and spices,

precious woods and precious oil and precious stones.

From his great riches he fortified his kingdom, sending workmen in every direction to enlarge palaces and build public buildings and raise grain silos. All was good and the people were happy and the king rested on his prosperity, until he, like his great-grandfather, forgot to look to the one beyond the sky and walk before the dawn with Light-Maker. In time he bowed to the golden calves as had so many northern kings before him.

The Reluctant Prophet wept at the broken promise and the foolishness that would soon destroy the kingdom. One morning as he stood before a stone altar, sacrificing a spotless, newborn lamb to the one who is infinite and eternal and all-powerful, a wind blew from the rising sun.

"Go to the great City of Blood in the Kingdom of the Bull," said the wind.

"But that is a wicked city," said the Reluctant Prophet. "Its people follow the ways of Shining One. They walk in darkness and violence and anarchy."

"They need someone to show them the light," whispered the wind.

"They do not deserve the light. They are the most brutal and ruthless and cruel people on the Blue Planet."

"That is true," said the wind. "So they above all others need you to show them the light. The light is for any who look beyond the sky, not just for those who deserve it."

"The Northern Kingdom is the bitterest of enemies to the People of the Bull," insisted the prophet, squinting his eyes as the wind blew strong and hot and dusty. "They have no mercy for their enemies. If I go to them, they will torture me and skin me alive and let me bake in the desert sun. They will impale my corpse on a wooden stake for the ravens to pick my bones clean. They will place my skull atop the city wall with the skulls of a thousand enemies who did not submit quickly enough."

"Will you fear if I go at your side? Will you fear if I walk before you into the city? Will you fear if I stand at your back? If I am with you, who will do you harm?"

"What if I go and the people do not listen to my words?"

"Their walls will fall into ruins, and those who remain alive will be led off into slavery."

One more question gnawed at the prophet.

"And if they hear my words and turn from their horrid ways? What if they look beyond the sky and cry out your name and sacrifice spotless, newborn lambs to you?"

"Then I will save their city and make of them a great nation."

The Reluctant Prophet said nothing, but his heart boiled inside him. That night, lying upon his bed, he muttered in the darkness what he had not dared say in the daylight to the desert wind: "I hate the City of Blood, and if they flourish, my people may perish. I will do nothing to save its people."

Yet now the night breeze blew through the window.

"I too hate all that they do," whispered the night breeze. "Yet I am Light-Maker and the giver of second chances. Go to them and show them my light."

The Reluctant Prophet got up from his bed and began walking. For two days he journeyed silently, stubbornly away from the City of Blood. When he reached the shore of the Great Sea, he found a small trading ship. He paid his passage and boarded the small vessel and felt the breeze fill its sail as it drifted toward the western edges of the Blue Planet.

CHAPTER 2

THE RELUCTANT PROPHET

Cut the sail!" cried the ship's master.

A mountain of water, almost as high as the single mast amidships crashed down upon the deck. Strong men strained at the great oars to steady their vessel and keep it pointed into the wind. The sky was twilight at midday, and the most seasoned sailors quaked as they frantically worked to strip away the tatters of the large square sail, gripping the ropes that kept them from being swept away with the next monstrous wave. Ships seldom survived such a gale as this. The men could do little more to keep their vessel afloat.

Dark clouds stole the sun.

Howling winds shoved the prow this way and that.

Mighty waves battered the hull.

Nothing seemed to steady the ship, and the storm grew more violent moment by moment. The sailors were exhausted and terror filled their hearts.

"Never have I seen such a storm on the Great Sea," shouted the master. "Cry out to Shining One to have mercy on us."

So the sailors pleaded with the ancient snake, promising all they had if he would only spare their lives. But the serpent could not hear their cries over the crashing waves. And even if he had heard, he could do nothing. For this was a storm from Light-Maker, and it would only stop at his word. He would not give that word until he had the attention of a tall, balding passenger, who at that moment was lying asleep belowdecks.

"Lighten the load," shouted the master as the wind stung his weathered face. The sailors moved quickly, throwing cargo into the churning maelstrom. But the ship settled lower and lower.

"Bring everybody on deck," said the master in desperation. "Especially that prophet who calls upon Light-Maker. Maybe he can save us."

"The prophet lies asleep," reported one of the sailors, who shook his head in wonder.

"Poor man must be dead or unconscious. No one sleeps through such a storm."

"I shook him. He opened his eyes and told me he did not want to be bothered. Then he turned over."

"Bring him at once!"

Soon the prophet stood before the master.

"This wind is from beyond the sky. Why does your Light-Maker wish to destroy us?"

The prophet looked out from the bucking deck in silence.

"Speak, or we shall all die."

The prophet stared at the master, but his mouth did not move.

The captain pushed the silent man back and shook his head. "There is no time. Bring the lots. Let us see who offends the one above all."

The lots were cast. The mark of guilt fell to Reluctant Prophet. All regarded him with angry muttering.

"Who are you?"

"What have you done?"

"Why is Light-Maker angry?"

"I am Reluctant Prophet," he said slowly, "and I am running from the one who is infinite and eternal and all-powerful. But I have not escaped the arm of Light-Maker."

"I follow Shining One, and I am no truth teller," answered the ship's master. "But I know enough not to try to run from Light-Maker. You must have done something evil indeed."

The prophet stood silent, and it seemed that the sky was even darker and the wind blew even harder and the waves were even higher, if that was possible.

"You are a truth teller for the one beyond the sky," said the master, his

23

voice strained with panic. "Tell the truth now. What can we do to appease his anger?"

"This is all my fault," said the prophet. "Throw me overboard. Then all will grow quiet."

"No man can survive such a raging sea," said the master. "I will not do that unless I have no other choice."

The men rowed with all their might in the direction of the shore. But the ship was tossed about with such fury that strong arms were useless.

"We have no choice," cried the weary men. "We are lost."

The captain looked beyond the sky and cried to the one above all. "Save us. What we do, we do out of awe and respect for your great power. Your prophet ran away and we return him to your hands."

As his words ended, the prophet was thrown to the waves.

In moments the wind ceased

and the swells calmed

and the ship rested on a sea of glass.

Reluctant Prophet could not be seen; already he was carried far from the ship in the grip of an outward current. In panic he fought his way toward the surface. But it was to no avail, for he could not swim, and the water pulled him downward. His lungs were bursting for breath, and he made one valiant final effort to push himself upward.

It was too late.

He faded into unconsciousness. He did not see the gigantic fish lunge at its prey nor its great jaws as they closed around him. He did not feel the jerk of its muscles as they pulled him in and in and farther in. The sharp teeth that ripped into the flesh of large prey had no more than grazed his leg. But now the muscles gave him a pummeling, squeezing the water from his lungs and forcing in gasps of dank, putrid air. He choked and breathed deep. The air was strong and stale and suffocating, but it sustained life. His lungs burned with the air. His skin burned from contact with the slime in which he lay. His eyes burned when he opened them, but he could see nothing. He reached out into the narrow tunnel of a cave—a cave with soft, slimy, throbbing walls. He cried out in horror and pulled back his hands.

"Oh, Light-Maker," called the Reluctant Prophet, "where am I?"

Over the next hours, when the walls weren't constricting around him, he slowly worked out an answer to his question. This thing around him was living. That much was obvious. He was inside it, so it had swallowed him. But he was alive. He felt no teeth gashes, and he had not been ground upon by molars. He had heard of great snakes that could swallow a man whole. But where could he have met one of those?

Now he remembered. The ship. The water. The bed of seaweed.

It was a fish. . . . It had to be. Could there be such a fish? Only from Light-Maker. Light-Maker had saved him from the storm.

Was this being saved? Yes, it must be. Light-Maker had not rejected him.

Deep in the heart of the sea.

Huddled in the belly of a fish.

Cold and wet and very sorry.

"Forgive me," wept Reluctant Prophet. "Save my life. I will do anything and say any message and go anywhere."

But it seemed Light-Maker was not ready to turn him loose, for he continued to be churned and pummeled. He still gasped for the little air available to breathe. Time went on until it seemed that there had been no time before he had made his bed in the soft tomb. All around him was wet, yet he was so thirsty. He struggled to move away from the burning acid exercising his aching muscles. He wondered what the fish was feeling about all of this.

Without warning he found out, for the muscles heaved and constricted ferociously, forcing him, feetfirst, back through the slippery tunnel and out past the murderous teeth. Cool water rushed over him, but he found a footing and discovered that he could stand. The water reached only to his waist. He staggered over the sharp rocks to the shore, not caring if they bruised or cut his feet. He lay amid the rocks on shore, deeply breathing the fresh air. He stood and wandered and found a stream of fresh water from which to drink. Then he fell into a dreamless sleep. A day and a night passed, and a hot morning wind blew from the east, awaking him.

"Go to the City of Blood," said the wind. "Show them the light."

"But. . ."

Reluctant Prophet closed his mouth. He said nothing more. He faced the wind and bowed his head and began walking slowly across the fertile crescent toward the Kingdom of the Bull.

Standing outside the strong walls of the City of Blood, Reluctant Prophet's heart was full of fear. This was a city owned by Shining One, a place known for violence and evil and anarchy.

Reluctant Prophet forced himself to enter the gates and walk the streets. He looked around and then beyond the sky.

He began shouting his message.

"If the people of the City of Blood do not look to Light-Maker, this place will stand no more."

The people stopped and listened to this horrifying prediction. News spread of the outsider with strangely white, scarred skin whose clothing hung in tatters. They talked about his startling words. Their eyes opened and their hearts softened and their lips finally admitted the greatness of the one who holds stars in his hands.

Reluctant Prophet had known that the people would not listen. They would ridicule and rebuke and chase him from their city. But instead they did listen. They bowed their heads and humbled themselves and begged for mercy. Even the governor stepped from his golden throne and shed his royal robe and sat in the midafternoon dust.

"Let us all look upon the majesty of Light-Maker," he commanded. "Reluctant Prophet is right. We must turn from the ways of Shining One. We must give up violence and evil and anarchy. Maybe then the one above all will have compassion upon us."

Light-Maker heard and smiled and had compassion. The City of Blood would stand for now.

"How could you do this?" cried Reluctant Prophet to the one beyond the sky. "This is a wicked city. Its people deserve to die."

"They have turned to me," whispered the wind.

"I hate them!" shouted the prophet as he stomped out of the city! "They are my enemy."

"But I made them. I love them," said the wind.

"I am your prophet, and my people are your people!" he shouted at the sky. "If you do not destroy this bloody city, then you might as well kill me."

"Why are you so angry?" asked the wind quietly.

The man clenched his jaw
and turned his back
and sat in the shade of a grape arbor.

He took off his sandals and rubbed his feet. He wiped the sweat that stung his scarred face. At least he could enjoy his shade. He plucked a handful of deep purple grapes and ate them one by one. Then he drifted into sleep.

As the sun lifted above the Mountains of the Dawn, Reluctant Prophet awoke to find that the arbor was shriveled and dead. A worm had burrowed into the vine and chewed away its heart. A scorching wind blew away the dry leaves.

"Why did you allow this beautiful vine with its broad leaves and succulent grapes to die?" demanded the prophet. "Don't you care about anything?"

"I care about many things," answered the wind. "I care about thousands of people who live in the City of Blood. Are you more concerned about your shade than the lives of an entire city?"

The Reluctant Prophet bowed his head in shame.

PROSPERITY IS AS TENUOUS
AS THE FUTURE.

CHAPTER 3

THE FARMER

The crops were bountiful.

The enemies stayed away.

The people grew wealthy.

The Northern Kingdom was as powerful as it had ever been, and Prosperous King was happy. Men collected many herds of cattle and the women purchased much jewelry and the children grew strong on fine food. And Shining One smiled as well, for he had coiled himself tightly around their hearts.

In the Southern Kingdom, in the howling hills above the City of Hope, stood a simple stone cottage surrounded by a small grove of sycamores. Inside lived a Farmer with a faithful wife and several young children. The Farmer was a strong man with callused hands and sunburnt face, like his father and grandfather before him. He worked his land and pruned his trees and watched his sheep. He was a poor and contented man who did not need wealth to make him happy.

Every morning as the sun crested the Mountains of the Dawn, the Farmer walked the dewy hills with the one who holds the stars in his hands. Where Light-Maker led, Farmer would follow. What the master said, the servant would do.

One morning, Farmer walked out of the hills and into the City of Palms. He stood silently in his ragged clothing before the splendor of the Special Place and he wept. Then he bent his head and sacrificed a spotless, newborn lamb to the one above all.

"Do you love me?" whispered the wind.

"With all my heart and soul and strength," said Farmer.

"Then journey to the Northern Kingdom. Go to the Place of the Portal where Schemer saw the angels walk the silver staircase."

Without hesitation, Farmer looked beyond the sky and traveled north. Days later he stood before the temple of the golden calf and shook his head in disgust.

"Why did you send me to this place?" asked Farmer. "Shining One holds their hearts and minds. Their ears are deaf. Their eyes are blind. They care nothing about what is right and good and pure."

"That is why I sent you," answered the wind. "I gave the City of Blood a chance and they followed me. My own people of the Northern Kingdom will have the same chance."

That night Farmer slept on the old straw of a simple stable floor, thinking of the beautiful crop that grew nearby in the king's fields. But as he slept, he also saw a million locusts swarming on the horizon, hungry to devour all that the land produced. As they began to sweep across the border, Farmer cried, "Show mercy to your people!"

The invasion stopped.

"I will show mercy," said the wind, "and hold back the locusts with my right hand."

The next morning Farmer went to the marketplace. He begged the people to look beyond the sky.

"Shining One clings to the darkness, but Light-Maker turns the darkness to dawn.

"He shaped the mountains.

"He directs the wind.

"He sets every future on its proper course.

"He wishes to save you from the ancient snake and the way of disaster."

"But we do not wish to be saved," said the crowd. "Shining One has made us rich and our riches make us happy."

Farmer hung his head and returned to his simple stable. That night, he dreamed again. This time he saw a cloudless sky and a burning sun. The springs diminished and the cattle grew thin and the crops withered. As the drought settled on the land, Farmer cried, "Show mercy to your people!"

At his prayer the clouds came.

"I will show mercy," said the wind, "and hold back the drought with my left hand."

The next morning Farmer went back to the marketplace and begged the people to reconsider.

"You say you are happy," said Farmer, "but your happiness will soon disappear. If you do not listen to the one above all, sadness will fill your days. Feasts will become funerals. Dancing will turn to dirges. Weeping will sweep the cities and fields and hills of the Northern Kingdom."

The people laughed and turned away and told the crazy man to return to the South.

Slowly Farmer walked back to his bed of straw. That night he dreamed a third dream. He saw a straight line, as straight as a cedar reaching for the sky. "The time has come to measure my people," said the wind. "I will lay my line beside their character. If they still refuse to turn to me, I will show them no more mercy.

"The Ivory Palace will be leveled.

"The temples will be destroyed.

"The Dynasty of the Sword will be no more."

The next morning Farmer returned to the temple of the golden calf. He pushed through the crowd of nobles who bowed to Shining One. He scooped up the coins they had set before the altar.

"You sell your innocence for a handful of silver!" shouted the rough farmer, throwing the coins into the air. "Money has become everything. Comfort has made you soft in the middle but hard in the heart."

"You have no right to say such things," said a large round man, the keeper of the dark temple.

"The ancient snake has blinded you with his foolish lies," said Farmer. "A little wine with a little music, and you have forgotten all that is true. Seek Light-Maker and he will show you what makes life meaningful."

"Look at yourself," laughed the dark keeper. "You have nothing but a worthless piece of land and the rags on your back. How dare you speak to us?"

"I have Light-Maker. That is worth more than all the silver and gold and precious jewels in the Northern Kingdom."

"Keep quiet and go home, or you will be dragged before the king." The keeper was losing his patience.

"I will speak with Prosperous King. He looks to his wealth, instead of the source of all wealth. He believes his kingdom is the greatest on the Blue Planet. But another day is coming.

"On this day the warrior will not be proud.

"On this day the archer will not stand.

"On this day the horseman will not escape.

"And when Light-Maker withdraws his hand of protection, even the king will be taken captive."

"You cannot speak so against the king," shouted the angry keeper, his face red with rage.

"If Light-Maker tells me to speak, I must speak. Even if my words are difficult and threatening and disturbing."

The dark keeper waved his hands in fury. "You shall die!" he screamed. "By the power of Shining One, you shall die."

Farmer smiled.

"Before I die, I will see the ancient snake swallow all that you know and own and treasure."

Farmer walked past the red-faced keeper and the curious crowd. He left the city and walked the highlands in the light of the full moon.

"They would not listen to me," said Farmer.

"I know," said the wind.

"They do not understand."

The wind was silent.

That night Farmer had another dream. A large woven basket was filled with grapes and apricots and figs. It looked beautiful until he drew near and saw many buzzing flies and breathed in the sickly sweet smell of spoilage.

"My people are ripe for destruction," said the wind, "and I will show no more mercy. They have planted fine vineyards, but they will not drink of the wine."

"What shall I do?" asked Farmer.

"Tell the people their future."

After the sun lifted above the Mountains of the Dawn, Farmer stood once more in the marketplace.

"A day of darkness comes. The Kingdom of the Bull will invade your land and crush your people and carry your children to a distant land. Your cities will fall and your fields will be burned and your vineyards uprooted."

"This will not be!" shouted back the people. "We are strong and secure. Our king is powerful and prosperous. No one can tear down our walls or defeat our warriors!"

"Only Light-Maker is invincible," said Farmer. "He alone is infinite and eternal and all-powerful."

"So Light-Maker threatens to destroy us?"

"You have chosen the way of the snake. You will learn the meaning of sorrow."

Prosperous King heard these words and ordered warriors to the Place of the Portal. "Arrest this man and bring him to me. If he resists, kill him."

That night Farmer had one more dream. He saw a wasteland of rubble and ruin. Wild animals roamed the hills and hardy weeds filled the fields. The land was still and empty and forsaken. But the most beautiful rainbow Farmer had ever seen arched across the sky.

"My people have turned from me, so I will remove my hands of protection. They will be crushed and carried to a distant land and know much sorrow. But there will be hope, for far in the future, Light-Maker will bring his people back to their land.

"They will rebuild their cities

"and again till their soil

"and replant their vineyards.

"In that day, they will see the light and look beyond the sky and remember the one who holds stars in his hands.

"I am always close and I will always care," said the wind.

Warriors circled the Place of the Portal. With swords drawn they pushed through the crowd. But when they reached the place where Farmer had taught the people, he was gone. They found no trace in all the city of the man who had spoken against the king.

Farmer was well on his way home to his stone cottage in the Southern Kingdom. He had said what Light-Maker had asked him to say. Now he headed toward the howling hills above the City of Hope.

He embraced his children and kissed his wife. He worked his land and pruned his trees and watched his sheep, just like before.

MERCIFUL LOVE
EMBRACES THOSE
WHO DESERVE
NEITHER MERCY NOR LOVE.

CHAPTER 4

THE FAITHLESS WIFE

Fire blazed in the soldier's eyes as he remembered the day.

"I wish we had caught him defaming our kingdom and king in the marketplace in front of all the people," he blustered in front of his wife. "How dare this foreigner come into our city and say such things."

Everywhere the talk was the same. Farmer had defamed the land and the people. Then he just disappeared into the South.

But there were those—the wife of the soldier among them—who saw the direction their king and people had taken. Yes, Farmer's condemnation had been harsh, but his words held truth.

One father told his family plainly that Farmer spoke truly and walked well with Light-Maker.

"Who is Light-Maker?" his son asked.

"He lives beyond the sky and holds the stars in his hands."

That night as the City on the Hill settled into its comfortable bed, the boy sat in the courtyard of his father's large house and watched the stars. How wondrous Light-Maker must be.

"How do I walk with you?" wondered the boy aloud.

"Listen to my words and follow my ways," answered the night wind.

The boy was startled by the unexpected voice, and he looked about. "Who is there?" he asked.

"I am the one you seek."

"You are Light-Maker?"

"That is one of my names."

"If you hold stars, how can you be near to me?"

"I am always close and I always care."

"I have heard the words of Farmer," said the boy. "Are they true?"

"He spoke my words. I tell the truth."

"Then you will destroy the City on the Hill?"

"They turned away to a golden calf. If they return and humble themselves, I will spare them."

"May I walk with you?"

"Arise before the sun touches the Mountains of the Dawn and follow my steps."

Before the city awoke, the boy left his father's house and walked the highlands with Light-Maker. His stride was short, but as he grew he could walk farther. His hands grew strong and his heart pure and his mind sharp. He was successful in the marketplace, selling exotic perfumes and fine silks and silver bangles.

One day in the earliest glint of the sun, Light-Maker said something odd.

"Will you follow wherever I lead?"

"Yes."

"And if I ask something that seems too hard?"

"Then you will give me strength and courage and compassion."

"I want you to marry the girl who stands on the street corner with the golden necklaces and rings and ankle bracelets."

"But she is. . ."

"We are discussing who *you* are," said the wind. "Will you follow?"

The Shopkeeper looked to the sky. His head swirled. If he married this woman, he would be disgraced. Could Light-Maker ask such a thing?

What if he answered "Yes"?

But what if he answered "No"?

He fell to his knees and tears filled his eyes, and his voice quivered.

"Yes," he responded.

The Shopkeeper could not remember when he first saw her—
Standing alone,
dressed seductively,

flirting with the night.

She seemed so young and beautiful, yet hard and sad as she flipped back her head, and her hair sparkled in the torchlight. Some said she was a priestess in the temple of Shining One, available to the men who worshiped there. Or she was the daughter of a priest who served the snake. Or she was simply an orphan who had made the only life for herself she could. It did not matter. She was an outcast.

Business had closed for the day when Shopkeeper slowly crossed the marketplace to where she stood. Stiffly, he introduced himself.

"I know who you are," she said with a smile.

"I have bread and cheese and a skin of wine. Will you join me for my evening meal?"

The girl looked at him, cautious and suspicious and uncertain. They strolled to the shade of a large sycamore. Over the meal they talked with surprising ease. He learned a little of her difficult life. She was different than he had expected.

After a long talk, the woman grew pensive and quietly regarded Shopkeeper.

"I have enjoyed our time together, but you have not answered my question. Why did you wish to meet me?" she asked.

"I wish to invite you to my wedding feast."

She looked down.

"That is kind, but your respectable friends would not think my presence appropriate."

"No, I'm sure they would not," he answered honestly. "But if it is you that I marry, then your presence is both appropriate and necessary."

"Can't you see their faces?" she said with a giggle. But her eyes narrowed when he did not share her laughter.

He spoke earnestly: "I do not think our marriage would be so funny."

Her eyes grew large. It was not her first offer of marriage, but it was the most unexpected.

"You are making fun of me," she accused.

"My offer is most serious."

"Do you know what I am? Do you know what I have done?"

"I know what you have done," said Shopkeeper gently. "But is it what you *are?* Look beyond the sky. Light-Maker will give you a new heart."

For a long moment she stared at the handsome young man. "Is this possible?"

"Anything is possible with the one above all."

Tears washed the paint from her face. "You can love me?"

He wiped tears from her eyes. "Of course, I can."

Within a cycle of the moon, they were married. It was a cause of amazement and amusement and even disgrace. But the entire city could not deny how happy the two seemed. They laughed and played and worked together. Before the sun rose above the Mountains of the Dawn, they even walked together with the one who holds stars in his hands.

In time she gave birth to a son. Light-Maker said, "Name him Broken; for if my people do not return to me, I will break them."

A summer later she bore a daughter. Light-Maker said, "Name her Pity; for all will pity those who bow to the golden calf."

Shopkeeper loved his wife and children. His business prospered, and all seemed well. But one day the ancient snake slipped into his home. He coiled in a corner and watched the wife care for her small children.

"You are not truly happy," he hissed.

"I am far happier than when I served you."

"But your husband works long hours. Your children are demanding. Remember the exciting, carefree days," continued the snake. "No responsibilities. No demands. No obligations. You were your own person. Now you are simply Shopkeeper's wife."

The next day she saw some former friends on the street corner. She stopped and flirted, and she found their attention appealing.

Her heart kept returning to that corner. One day, for fun, she painted her face and put on her golden jewelry and joined them. They introduced her to an older man with broad shoulders and dark eyes. He listened to her and complimented her beauty.

That night Shopkeeper knew something was wrong. His wife was silent, and her smile gone. She pulled away when he put his arms around her and looked into her eyes.

"I do not feel well," she stammered.

"Is there anything I can do?" asked Shopkeeper.

"Nothing," she said with a distant sigh.

The next day the man with the broad shoulders led her to his house, where desire succumbed to passion. That night she seemed more distant and had no smile for Shopkeeper.

Her face turned away.

Her heart grew cold.

Her every thought was for another.

No matter how kind and gentle and loving he was, the barrier grew higher between them. Once she left her children with a neighbor and disappeared for days. She returned with no explanation for her husband.

Shopkeeper looked beyond the sky and asked, "What shall I do?"

"Care for her," said the wind. "Ask her to humble herself and return her heart to her home."

"What you ask is hard," said Shopkeeper.

"Then put your heart in my hand," said the wind. "I never ask what cannot be done."

So Shopkeeper took the hand of the one above all and loved his wife as before. Yet her heart remained far away. As harvest changed to planting time, the faithless wife felt movement in her body. A tiny infant warmed her womb, and she knew it was not her husband's.

When she bore a son, Light-Maker said, "Name him Stranger; for my people have become strangers to me."

But suddenly the faithless wife and her newborn were gone. Shopkeeper knew where she had gone, and he knew why. But in the house of the man with the broad shoulders she found neither love nor peace nor acceptance. This man beat and belittled her, then he tied her and sold her to another man.

The people of the City on the Hill felt heartsick for Shopkeeper. They brought him food and advice. But his response stunned them: "Look at my unfaithful wife and see yourselves and our nation. How are you any better? You are the People of the Promise who belong to Light-Maker. But you live with Shining One.

"You cling to your prosperity

"and dance in the darkness

"and bow to your golden calf.

"Cry not for me but for yourselves. Your prosperity will fade and the Kingdom of the Bull will charge into our fields. Sound the trumpets and shout
the warnings."

"Why do you threaten us?" someone asked.

"I speak the words of Light-Maker," said Shopkeeper. "When he is angry,
he roars like a mighty lion seeking someone to devour. Wash the paint from
your face. Brush the sparkles from your hair. Pull the jewelry from your
ears. You have played the prostitute long enough. If you do not return, the
lion will fall upon your kingdom.

"No more smiles.

"No more laughter.

"No more celebration.

"Outsiders will drive you from your land. You will be homeless wander-
ers, lost and ruined."

"Is there no hope?" asked an old man.

"There is always hope with Light-Maker," said the loving husband.
"Turn your face to the sky. The maker of all saved the City of Blood. He
will forgive your unfaithfulness and embrace you."

"But how can he accept us if we have forsaken him?" asked the old man.

Shopkeeper smiled. "Watch."

He went into his house and returned with a bag of silver and a sack of
barley. The crowd followed him through the marketplace to the house
of the burly man who owned his faithless wife. He pounded on the door
and the man appeared, angry but a little afraid at seeing so many people
crowded in the street. Quietly he spoke with Shopkeeper. They agreed on
a price, and the man carried the grain and the silver inside. He shoved the
bruised girl into the street with a laugh. "Take her if you want her."

Shopkeeper bent down and wiped the tears from her eyes. He brushed the
dust from her dress and kissed her forehead. He took the frightened baby
from her arms and held it close. Then he looked into the faces about him.

"See what Light-Maker is willing to do. Now go home and think about
what I have said. I must speak with my wife."

Shopkeeper gently touched the trembling chin and guided her gaze from the dust until she looked into his eyes.

"You are free to do whatever you wish," he said. "If you return to our home, you will be my wife and I will be your husband."

"You could never forgive me," she whispered.

"You are already forgiven."

He held her child as they walked slowly toward their home. In time, they laughed and played and worked together once more. They even walked together once again with the one who holds stars in his hands.

The people of the City on the Hill watched, amazed. They saw the unfaithful wife return, but only a few followed her example. The rest refused to return to the one who loved them.

VIOLENCE MAY END
A PROBLEM,
BUT IT DOESN'T GUARANTEE
A SOLUTION.

⟐

CHAPTER 5

THE DECLINE

Shall we kill him?" asked the soldiers.

"Let him be," said Prosperous King.

"But he says the Kingdom of the Bull is a threat to our security."

"Maybe Shopkeeper is right," said the king with a sigh. "Maybe we are as faithless as his wife was. Maybe we should humble ourselves before Light-Maker before it is too late."

"Don't trouble yourself so, my dear king," said a snake who had been listening quietly beneath the royal throne. "For over forty summers I have given you wealth and power and prosperity beyond your greatest expectations. Why would you want anything else?"

"Many summers ago, I promised Reluctant Prophet that I would follow Light-Maker and never bow to the golden calves. But I have broken my promises. Riches distracted me from doing what I know is right, and now I realize my foolishness."

"You are just tired and old and feebleminded," said the snake with a mocking laugh. Then the serpent regarded the look of anger on the king's face and realized that he had said too much. He spoke more gently. "You have lived long and served well. There is no need to regret anything. Sit back and enjoy your final days."

"You have lied to me all along. I know that now. I can see that the words of Farmer and Shopkeeper are true.

"Fields are wilting.

"Riches are fading.

"Enemies stand at our borders."

"You simply need a rest. Leave the kingdom to my care for awhile."

"You take me for a fool. The Northern Kingdom is on the edge of decline and unless we do something quickly, it will be too late."

"It is never too late," said the snake. "Give me one more summer, and if the kingdom does not improve, then turn to Light-Maker if you think he can save you."

So the king, who was so very tired, did nothing. Before the year was over, Prosperous King grew weak and his breath shallow, and then his heart was still. A cry went out from the Ivory Palace that brought tears to all within the City on the Hill. Most had known no other king. He was buried in grand style beside his father and grandfather and great-grandfather.

The following day his firstborn son was given the crown and sat on the golden throne. But he was a proud man who loved his riches more than anything else. He did not share his father's ways. He ignored the one above all and followed the ways of the snake and bowed to the golden calves.

The new king saw that his kingdom was not as prosperous as before, so he made the people work harder. They increased the harvest and expanded the flocks and fortified the cities. The king was happy, but his people were angry; and some even plotted against the throne.

On a breezy day, the king entered the Valley of Harvest on his way to the Summer Palace. He led the way on a magnificent white stallion with bodyguards on his left and right. Close behind moved several wooden wagons, carrying his wife and small children. The sky was a light blue, and the breeze made the midday heat bearable. The king was lost in thought about how he could keep his kingdom great. The wife rocked an infant and sang an ancient lullaby. The children slept peacefully and dreamed the dreams of innocence.

Suddenly two arrows sailed from the nearby rocks. One pierced the heart of the guard at the right of the king, and the other pierced the heart of the guard at the left. Both gasped and slumped and fell lifeless from their horses. More arrows rained upon the small caravan as a band of assassins rushed out of the hills with cries of fury.

The king pulled his sword and turned back to protect his family. But it was too late. Several large men had surrounded the wagons and already were killing his wives with swift sword thrusts. Children screamed and held onto each other in terror. The remaining royal guards fought valiantly, but the force against them was large and they could not stand.

A large man with long brown hair raised his sword. "Kill the children," he yelled. "Save the king for me."

"No!" shouted the king in rage as he galloped toward the wagon.

The leader with the long brown hair deftly parried the wild swing of the king's sword. The stallion reared, and strong hands pulled the king from his horse. Stirred by fear and wrath, the king regained his footing and charged into the man with long brown hair. He fought valiantly, trying to force his way to the wagons, from which he could hear the screams of his dying children. As his last child was cut down, the king dropped his sword in despair. The lead assassin laughed as he swung his blade at the head of his king. Blood covered the ground as the man with the long brown hair lifted his arms in triumph. "I am the new king. I am the king of the Northern Kingdom."

The reign of the Sword Dynasty was over. It had begun in violence and so did it end. The kingdom was in shock. They had hated the man who had ruled over them for only six cycles of the moon, but they were appalled at this brutal murderer of the royal family who now proclaimed that he was over them. However, believing they had no choice, the people grudgingly accepted the Assassin King. But a day to the west a fierce general in charge of a mountain garrison fumed. He had spent his entire life loyal to Prosperous King, and he refused to acknowledge this murderer as anything more than a common criminal with delusions of grandeur. He gathered his warriors and asked where they stood.

"Do any of you support this impostor?"

"No!" came a mighty cry.

"Then what shall we do?" asked the general.

"Attack him and remove his crown."

"But who shall be the next king?"

"He stands before us," shouted his faithful men.

The next day the general marched toward the rising sun and attacked the City on the Hill.

He stormed the unguarded gates

and pushed past the surprised defenses

and forced his way into the Ivory Palace.

"How dare you enter the king's court with such violence?" declared Assassin King.

"That is the way you came here," said the general as he pulled his sword from its sheath.

The king called for help, but no one came.

"You are no king," continued the general as he walked unhesitatingly forward with the point of his sword aimed at the murderer's heart.

His victim backed up, stuttering and stammering, until he was pressed against the far wall.

"You cannot do this!" yelled the king with a sudden surge of rage.

His voice was cut off as the blade passed through his body with such force that the point drove deep into the wooden paneling behind him.

The king groaned and bled out his life. The general pulled free his sword and walked from the palace, holding high his scarlet blade under the sparkling sky.

"Long live the General King!" shouted the warriors and the gathering city folk, who had quickly seen the importance of what was happening.

General King was popular, and he brought a period of cautious peace to his people. But across the fertile crescent, beyond the Great River, the Kingdom of the Bull was growing restless. It threatened every surrounding kingdom with its mighty army and its giant siege machines and its insatiable hunger for land.

The new king immediately began to prepare for the invasion he knew was coming soon. He reinforced the eastern frontier, and he killed the leaders of any town that was unwilling to pledge its utmost loyalty to the Northern Kingdom. Within a cycle of the moon, every city declared its enthusiastic willingness to stand with their new king. All too soon, the King of the Bull crossed the Great River and invaded the Northern Kingdom with a force like an unstoppable swarm of locusts. The savage army spread across the land all the way to the City on the Hill and the Great Sea.

General King knew that he was lost if he fought on the battlefield. He asked for a truce and faced Bull King. An agreement was forged. The invaders would retreat and leave the Northern Kingdom unharmed if an annual tribute was paid of a bag of silver for every prosperous man within its boundaries.

The people paid.

The invaders left.

The king bowed to the golden calves in thanksgiving.

And Light-Maker shook his head in sorrow. The Northern Kingdom thought its safety was assured. The people were oblivious to the destruction hovering on the horizon.

DEFIANCE BEGS A RESPONSE.
ONE MUST BE PREPARED
TO EITHER DEFEND OR FACE DEFEAT.

CHAPTER 6

THE INVASION

General King kept a fragile peace. As long as all paid their bag of silver, the Kingdom of the Bull did not cross the Great River.

When the king died, the people feared the end of peace. The king's son took the throne and declared that he would continue all his father had begun. He met with the Bull King and declared that he would honor the agreement made by his father. The Northern Kingdom sighed in relief that their lives would not be threatened.

However, on the east bank of the Winding River rose a warrior with hate in his heart. He was determined to spurn and resist and fight the Kingdom of the Bull. He was disgusted by the negotiations of General King's son.

One bright afternoon the warrior stood on the stairs of the Ivory Palace and cried out:

"Why should we talk to such an enemy?"

"Why should we give away our silver?"

"Why should we cower?"

"There are many things you do not understand," replied the king.

"What we understand," said the defiant warrior, "is that you will not stand strong against those who threaten our kingdom."

"But I have maintained the peace of my father."

"You empty our land of all its silver, just as your father did," said the warrior. "What will you do when there is nothing left to give?"

The king was silent.

The warrior spat on the steps and turned his back and returned to the east bank. There he traveled from city to city, speaking of the cowardice of the king. He gathered a group of young men with courage.

"We do not have to hide in fear from the Bull Kingdom!" he shouted. "Come to my side and let us confront the king. If he will not join our cause, we will go to battle without him."

A cycle of the moon later, the defiant warrior crossed the Winding River with fifty fighting men. They marched into the highlands and to the gates of the City on the Hill.

"We wish to meet with our king," demanded the warrior.

"The king cannot be disturbed," replied the keeper of the gate.

"But this is urgent."

The keeper sent a runner to the Ivory Palace, who returned with the king's own words: "I am feasting with friends and have no desire to meet with you today. Make an appointment for tomorrow or the day after, and I will consider your concerns."

The warrior swore at the sky and shoved the runner to the ground and grabbed the tunic of the gatekeeper. Grasping the clothing of the trembling man, he shouted into his face, "Take me to the king!"

"I cannot do that."

The warrior lifted the man off his feet and threw him violently against the city wall. The man's head struck the mortared stones with a heavy thud, and he fell, lifeless, to the ground.

"Follow me!" the warrior shouted to his men.

As they passed through the gate, several guards stepped forward to block their way. Without hesitation, the defiant warrior pulled his sword and swung it into the startled guards, killing them before a cry could be sounded.

The fighting men marched to the Ivory Palace and killed the royal bodyguards and burst into the grand banquet hall.

Women screamed.

Men shouted.

People scattered.

Bolting the door behind him, the warrior jumped upon a heavy oak table and yelled above the din of the guests. "We demand to be heard by the king!"

General King's son stepped forward with eyes blazing and fire in his voice.

"Why should I speak to violent ruffians?"

"If you will not hear us, we will take the breath from every person in this room."

"So you break into my palace and threaten your king? What has become of the kingdom?"

"The kingdom has become poor and broken and desperate," said the defiant warrior. "We wish a king with the courage to face our enemy."

"Negotiations sometimes take more courage than a bloody sword."

"Negotiations that fill the treasury of an enemy with our hard-earned silver betray the kingdom. We will no longer bow to a king who bends to the enemy. We refuse to pay a single silver coin to those who threaten us."

"Then we will be crushed, and our people will lie dead in the streets or be carried off to lands beyond the Mountains of the Dawn."

"Then we will form an alliance with the kingdoms around us. Together we can stand against our enemy and break his power over us."

The king laughed loudly. He stepped closer and held his middle as the laughter rolled without restraint. "The other kingdoms are weaker than we are. The Kingdom of the Bull will laugh at the army we all can field together. Your idea is foolish."

The defiant warrior was enraged. With a flash of his sword, he plunged his weapon into the king's chest. The guests looked on in stunned silence as their ruler dropped to the floor in a pool of his own blood.

The fifty fighting men encircled the warrior and placed the golden crown on his head and declared him the Defiant King of the Northern Kingdom. All the guests bowed low, out of fear rather than loyalty.

Defiant King quickly took control of the kingdom and severed all agreements with the Kingdom of the Bull. When the time came to send their bags of silver, none were sent. The king organized an alliance of kingdoms to stand as one against the powerful bull. The King of the City of Caravans and the King of the Plains People and the King of the Sea People all joined with the Northern Kingdom, but the Southern Kingdom refused. The Defiant King explained and pleaded and threatened, but his brothers to the South stood their ground.

"We too have an agreement with the Kingdom of the Bull," said the

Southern King, "and we will continue to pay our tribute with bags of silver."

"But if you join us, we will have more power to resist the armies of our enemy."

"We have no desire to join you."

"Then you will die first."

The following spring the alliance of four attacked the Southern Kingdom. They took the land and burned the fields and shattered the cities—every city except the City of Palms, which stood strong against the army of the alliance.

They killed the valiant warriors.

They captured the wives and children.

They gathered a great deal of plunder.

A lengthy line of captives and cattle and wagons full of all that held value strung across the landscape. Northward they marched to the City on the Hill. But before they passed through the gates, a man of truth stepped forward and blocked their way.

"Light-Maker allowed you to win this battle as a lesson to the Southern Kingdom," he shouted. "But he will not allow you to enslave his people as your servants."

Defiant King stared unblinkingly into the truth teller's eyes and declared, "The law of war says we can take whatever we wish."

"But the law of light says that if you ignore the words of the one above all, you will suffer great loss."

"So what are the words of the one above all?" asked the king with a derisive laugh, as he stepped back from the man of truth.

"Quickly return every captive to the land from which they were taken."

The king blustered. "I will instead enslave you as well."

"Please, my king," interrupted one of his most respected leaders. "Many of us still fear the one who is above all, and he has declared that we must not make slaves of our brothers. We dare not anger him as we face a terrible army. The men will lose heart at the truth teller's words if you do not listen. We have taken much plunder. Let us return these captives to their land."

Defiant King reluctantly agreed. The captives were each given good food and fresh water and new sandals. They were escorted two days south to the Fortress City and released. Yet the king was still bent on punishing the Southern Kingdom for not joining his alliance against the tyranny of the bull.

The next spring the armies of Defiant King and Caravan King surrounded the City of Palms.

They pounded the walls

and stormed the gates

and cut off the city from outside help.

But late one night a runner crept through the secret tunnels that carried water to the city. Once beyond the walls and warriors, he set his face to the northeast. With a royal scroll clutched in his hands, he moved swiftly through the highlands and across the Winding River. Quickly he reached the Kingdom of the Bull.

"My city is under siege. The alliance that has spurned your tribute is trying to destroy my kingdom because I remain obedient. I am your humble servant, and my people have paid their bags of silver faithfully. If you will save my city, I will reward you from the wealth held within the splendid sanctuary and the royal palace."

The King of the Bull smiled in savage delight as he read the scroll. This was better than he had imagined. Now he could attack and plunder those who resisted him, while being paid handsomely by his vassals.

Soon his army of locusts crossed the Great River and swarmed toward the City of Caravans. When they heard of his invasion, Defiant King and Caravan King gave up their siege and marched to protect their people.

For Caravan King it was too late. When he came within sight of his city, he saw billowing smoke darken the sky and broken masses of people scattering across the land.

He led his courageous warriors toward the open jaws of the bull in vain heroism. By evening the king and all his men were dead. The next day the city was ransacked and its people were captives. They would become slaves in some distant corner of the ruthless kingdom.

Then the mighty army marched on. It easily captured the lands east of the Winding River. It swept through the lands surrounding the Stormy Sea and the coastal lowlands. All the mountains and valleys and rivers of the Northern Kingdom were claimed by the enemy, everything except the City on the Hill.

Defiant King sat in his Ivory Palace and cursed the one who holds the stars. His mighty men strengthened the city walls and waited for the attack. Now they knew the truth. It was exactly as Farmer and Shopkeeper had predicted.

The invasion had come.

The kingdom had fallen.

The people were prisoners.

Defiant King could rant and rave and scream at the sky, but the end was near.

It was only a matter of time.

COLLAPSE IS INEVITABLE
IF ONE DEPENDS ON PHYSICAL STRENGTH
TO THE EXCLUSION OF MORAL CHARACTER.

CHAPTER 7

THE COLLAPSE

"How well do you know your Defiant King?" asked the Bull King.

"We grew up not far from each other in the Northern Kingdom," answered the bound soldier who bowed so low before him that his face nearly touched the ground. "We served together in the army and became close friends."

"Do you agree with his military strategies?"

"No, he is a proud man, who is destroying the kingdom. There is great foolishness in a field mouse who puts on his armor to fight a lion."

"Well said. So what do you suggest?"

"We should stop resisting and return to the ways of General King. We should each pay our bag of silver and be thankful that you do not ask for more."

"I like you," bellowed the Bull King, and he ordered the man unbound and offered him a seat at his royal table in the City of Blood. "You know how to evaluate a situation without letting your pride get in the way."

"Pride helps no dead man."

"So what if you were the next king of the Northern Kingdom?" asked Bull King.

"Defiant King is strong and healthy," replied the soldier.

"But a smart warrior who is friends with the king could get close enough to see that he becomes much less healthy," said Bull King. "Then you could be king and save your kingdom from the foolishness of its current path. Not only would you be a hero, but I would make you the wealthiest man in the New Land."

The soldier smiled as he considered the possibilities. It certainly wasn't that he was being offered riches to betray his country. He would be the people's savior.

Several cycles of the moon later, the soldier was sitting with Defiant King in a private chamber of the Ivory Palace.

A feast.

A jug of wine.

A dagger thrust into the heart.

Defiant King grabbed his chest with shock and pain shining in his eyes. A gurgle came from his throat as he slumped in his chair and fell facefirst upon the floor.

Now looking at the body surrounded by blood, the soldier was horrified. Somehow he had expected to feel more triumph at this moment. "What have I done?" he asked, transfixed by the body of his friend lying before him.

"You have joined the fraternity of violence and greed and anarchy," answered a snake that crawled across the banquet room and over the vacant face of the dead king.

The soldier looked away from the corpse, and the serpent came near.

"No, do not feel guilt. You have succeeded in doing a great thing for the kingdom," hissed the voice. "You have saved the people from destruction and begun a new dynasty. You are my brother. Now let us bow before the golden calves so that your reign might be prosperous and powerful and long."

The new king did everything the snake said. The Northern Kingdom was small and feeble as it rested in the shadow of the mighty bull. Yet the new king made sure that all paid their bag of silver so that the Army of the Bull would let his kingdom exist.

However, as the summers passed, silver became scarce, and people complained at how difficult it was to pay the tribute.

"We cannot do this any longer," cried out the people of the City on the Hill. "We have become poor and powerless."

"But if we resist the Kingdom of the Bull," said the Desperate King, "they will crush us."

"Not if we seek help," said the people.

So the king considered all. He spoke to the wisest people in the Northern

Kingdom, and they told him of the ancient scrolls. His counselors reminded him of the stories of Reluctant Prophet and Farmer and Shopkeeper. He thought long and hard about Light-Maker.

Did he truly live beyond the sky?

Could he hold the stars in his hands?

Was it possible for him to be infinite and eternal and all-powerful?

"It is all a foolish fable," whispered the snake. "The only ones who believe such stories are children and old women."

"But we need help," said the king.

"I can give you all the help you need," smiled the snake. "Bow low to the golden calves and look deep into my eyes."

Again the king did everything the snake said.

As another summer passed, the people complained more loudly.

"What shall I do?" the king asked the snake.

"Send runners to the King of the Delta and sell yourselves to his kingdom if he will protect you against the onslaught of the bull."

"But then we will be his slaves."

"Not at all," assured the snake. "It's simply an alliance. He helps you, and when he needs help, you help him."

"But. . ."

"Don't worry. You can trust him."

So runners were sent to the King of the Delta, and an agreement was made. When the time came for the Northern Kingdom to pay its tribute, no bags of silver were gathered.

Bull King was furious. He sent his mighty army across the Great River toward the City on the Hill. Desperate King sent runners to the Land of the Delta to tell them that it was time for them to come and help.

But no one came. The Army of the Bull marched closer, and the king sent for help a second time. Still no one came.

"We are about to be crushed," cried out the king. "What shall we do?"

"Do not worry," said the snake. "The Kingdom of the Bull looks powerful, but it will not harm you. All they want is their tribute. So gather all the bags of silver and ride out to meet the army."

So Desperate King loaded bags of silver on many, many beasts of burden.

Then he mounted the finest stallion in the kingdom and led the beasts with silver on their backs through the city gates. When Bull King saw Desperate King, he laughed out loud.

"Capture the king and tie his hands and bring him to me," said Bull King. "Take the tribute and send it to the City of Blood."

"I have come to deliver your bags of silver," said Desperate King as he stood before his master. "So why have you taken me captive?"

"You know what you have done," said Bull King. "Because you have brought your silver, I will not take your life. But you shall no longer be king, and your kingdom shall no longer be free."

The warriors seized him and blindfolded him and took him beyond the Mountains of the Dawn. There he was thrown into a prison in a small town and left to die.

"Surround the city and storm the gates!" shouted Bull King.

Desperate King had prepared the City on the Hill for such an attack.

Water supplies had been secured.

Food had been stockpiled.

Walls had been reinforced.

So when the Army of the Bull seized the city, its people were neither surprised nor depressed. The only thing that dismayed them was the capture of their king.

For three long years the army camped around the city and blocked it from any contact with the rest of the Blue Planet. For three long years the people of the city stayed within their walls and hoped their enemy would give up. Every day the Army of the Bull assaulted the walls and attacked the gates, but by nightfall the army returned to its tents unsuccessful.

But time was on the side of the invaders. Wells ran dry and even stockpiled food ran out. Spirits fell. Those within the walls grew tired and weak and hopeless. Then one day as the Army of the Bull assaulted the city, the gates splintered and the people surrendered and the kingdom collapsed.

All the people of the City on the Hill were taken captive and sent away to lands at the foot of the Mountains of the Dawn. There they settled and lived and ultimately died.

Bull King smiled at his successful campaign.

The king was his.

The Northern Kingdom was his.

The People of the Golden Calf were his.

Those in the South shook their heads in sadness at the fate of their brothers. They knew that this had happened because the Northern Kingdom had turned its back on the one beyond the sky. The Northern Kingdom had loved its golden calves while they hated or ignored or misused the words of the one who holds stars in his hands. They had followed the ways of Shining One—ways of violence and greed and anarchy. Now those ways led to collapse and captivity.

Those in the South also were disobedient to Light-Maker, but they had listened to the words of hope. Even in the midst of great disobedience, many knew about the ancient promise of the rainbow: He is always close and he will always care.

But there was also a new promise. The people looked high into the night and searched the sky for the stars with the greatest fire. These were the stars that reminded them of a new promise: No matter how dark the path, he will always show the way.

Tears marked each face, for many people believed the truth tellers when they said that the path ahead was indeed dark. But the truth tellers also declared that at the end of the path was the brightest of all the lights that Light-Maker had ever made.

EPILOGUE

The week had begun with the tears of the old man.

As they had listened to the stories each night, the people around the circle had also cried with Farmer and Shopkeeper. The North was no more, and no amount of crying could bring back the nation or its people. The time had come to dry tears.

Now as the week ended with its stories of Light-Giver, the evening's fire was beginning to burn low. The people still watched the ancient storyteller, for he might have more to teach this night. The old man with a hundred wrinkles turned silently to watch the people whose faces were turned toward him. Then he raised his walking stick and pointed to the sky. Every eye looked up to where a thousand diamonds sparkled in a brilliant canopy of beauty and hope. Each person contemplated the promise of Light-Maker, except the young children who snuggled cozily asleep on their parents' laps. The old man stood slowly and slipped from the dwindling light to walk for awhile into the western wilderness.

"Grandfather, Grandfather," came the call of the nine-year-old girl child as she ran to clasp his hand. She looked into his eyes, which seemed to sparkle even in the vague moonlight.

"Why the stars?" she asked simply. The man thought for a moment, then he bent low and whispered so softly that she could barely hear.

"He is Light-Maker."

The old man paused, and the girl waited.

"Wise King said that light is better than darkness." The man stood up and looked toward the sky. The girl looked up as well.

"He was a smart man, wasn't he?" she said.

"He certainly was," the old man said with a smile and a gentle pat on her back.

PART 2
THE COMFORT-GIVER

TABLE OF CONTENTS
THE COMFORT-GIVER

Prologue 61

1. The Leper King (2 Kings 15:1–7; 2 Chronicles 26) 63

2. The Writer (2 Kings 15:32–38; 2 Chronicles 26:21–27:9;

    Isaiah 5–6) 69

3. The Fire King (2 Kings 16; 2 Chronicles 28; Isaiah 5–12) 75

4. The Committed King (2 Kings 18–20; 2 Chronicles 29–32) . . 81

5. The Uncommitted Kings (2 Kings 21; 2 Chronicles 33) 87

6. The Book King (2 Kings 22:1–23:30; 2 Chronicles 34–35;

    Jeremiah 1–3) 93

7. The Prophet Haters (2 Kings 23:31–24:16;

    Jeremiah 19–20, 22, 26, 36) 99

8. The Final King (2 Kings 24:17–25:1;

    Jeremiah 27, 29, 34, 37–38, 51 105

9. The Broken City (2 Kings 25; Jeremiah 39–40, 52;

    Lamentations) 111

Epilogue 116

PROLOGUE

Soon it would be the season of lambing, and ewes heavy with their unborn bleated near the firelight. They were kept close, for even under the watchful care of the night watchman, the expectant mothers were vulnerable and easily spooked. Panic-stricken runs could bring disaster for a mother near her time. The old man whose sandled feet aimlessly circled the fire, stopped and listened to their gentle protests.

"Listen to the cries of the Southern Kingdom," he said softly. "Hear the cries of the City of Palms as they approached the moment when judgment gave birth. How sad they sound."

The shepherds and their wives looked to the northwest, their thoughts fixed on the ancient capital with its sacred sanctuary—the very center of life for the People of the Promise.

"Once more we turn to the history of our people, for we are the People of the Promise, and what you are about to hear happened to our ancestors."

The people thought of the pain their nation had endured and the calamity that had fallen upon their city of cities. All was hushed but for the ewes.

"It is a difficult time now," said the man of a hundred wrinkles. "It was hard then as well." The fire glow illuminated the nods of agreement. A desert owl's call mixed in with the bleating sheep, and a nearby fox added its cry.

"Listen to the predators in search of prey.

"Listen to the fearful in search of comfort.

"But listen more closely and you shall hear the wind.

"Only in the voice of the one above all was there hope. For those who listened and looked beyond the sky, there was a promise. For the rest, there was nothing."

The old man stopped and closed his eyes and listened. He felt the gentle night breeze touch his face. And he began to tell of Leper King.

PRIDE CAN TAKE ONE DOWN
WITH A SINGLE BLOW.
FAITH CAN LIFT ONE UP
WITH A SINGLE TOUCH.

CHAPTER 1

THE LEPER KING

The Southern Kingdom looked beyond the sky and walked with the one who holds stars in his hands. When it faced the Mountains of the Dawn, it feared neither the Kingdom of the Bull nor the Kingdom of the Dragon. When the Northern Kingdom threatened its borders, it did not flinch.

The king's son was small but strong, with broad shoulders and sinewy arms. A mere sixteen summers had left a deep mark of maturity on his face. The City of Palms noted that there was a look of authority and compassion in his eyes. The young man was shown respect wherever he walked. In return he showed respect to all he met.

When his father was imprisoned in the Northern Kingdom by the father of Prosperous King, the young man was immediately crowned.

"How can I rule," he asked his mother, "when I have so little experience?"

"Rise before the day and walk the highlands with Hope-Giver. Listen to his words and he will show you the way."

The young king did as his mother said. The one above all brought blessings to the Southern Kingdom.

The crops were fruitful.

The cattle were bountiful.

The country was as content as ever before.

As the king walked the hills and meadows and forests of his kingdom, he gained new appreciation for all the wonders of creation. He sat beside a gurgling brook, watching a doe drink deeply. The doe looked about in alert confidence, then drank again. The young man smiled. Cupping his hands, he too drank from the clear, cool water. The morning wind smelled of fresh honeysuckle. Hawks screamed from a light blue sky before reaching their perch atop a giant oak.

Everywhere he went the boy soaked in the beauty of nature. Some days it was the brilliant colors of wild lilies and roses. Other days brought to his ears the harsh roar of a lion or the soft cooing of a turtledove. Every day was filled with something new: an interesting texture, a stimulating taste, a pungent smell. His young heart never forgot to find amazement in these things, for each day was different. Each day was marvelous.

Of all his journeys into the surrounding countryside, his favorite memory was of the moment he descended into the Valley of Apples. The place sparkled with snow-white apple blossoms. As a light breeze swept through the trees, a thousand delicate flowers broke free and danced in joyful abandon—until the wind stilled and each exhausted dancer fell gracefully to the ground. He strolled through ancient orchards of fig and olive, running his hand along their gnarled trunks. He wandered the carefully kept vineyards, sampling from the large clusters of perfectly shaped fruit. He set a single purple grape in his mouth, rolling it about once or twice before biting through its skin. The juice was as sweet and savory as anything he had ever tasted.

"This is paradise," he said to the maker of all.

"As all the land should be," whispered the wind. "You are glimpsing the life I gave to Man and Woman before they made their fatal choice. Someday the Blue Planet will be like this once again."

Wandering across the gardenlike valley, the young king came to a field where tender, green growth had pushed its way through the ground. Rain had just freshened the land, so the sandy soil he scooped up felt moist to the touch. He rubbed it between his fingers and brought a pinch of it to his nose. Breathing deeply of its rich earthy smell, he smiled.

I would much rather be a farmer than a king, he thought to himself, sighing at the irony of a king feeling that way.

"There is not so great a difference between farmers and kings," said his mother when he remarked to her of his experience. "Both have the task of caring for the land that Hope-Giver has made. The fields do not belong to the king or the farmer. We are caretakers of what belongs to the one beyond the sky. If we do our jobs well, the land prospers. If we fail to fulfill our responsibilities, the land withers."

Soon the young king had little time to walk the valleys or listen to the hawks, for he had to be a king. He trained a powerful army with swords and spears, bows and armor, slings and shields. With this mighty force, he battled the Sea People and the Plains People. He stretched the boundaries of his nation from the Great Sea to the Coral Sea, from the Northern Kingdom to the Land of the Deltas. He spread his influence until his name was known by kings throughout the Blue Planet.

He fortified his towns on the western lowlands and raised tall, stone towers in the desert. He strengthened and enlarged the walls of the City of Palms so that it could withstand attack. Then he rebuilt Harbor Town, which had served the nation as a port under Sailor King a hundred years before.

His kingdom was grand and his people happy, but the southern king longed to touch the land. He spent every spare moment with those who worked the fields and tended the vineyards and cared for the orchards. He learned all he could about what the best soils were like and what could be produced in them. He dug cisterns throughout his kingdom to catch the precious rain. He cleared more land of rock, until the arid nation bloomed to an extent many had thought impossible, even to the edge of the wilderness.

During all the early days of his reign, the king walked with the one who holds stars in his hands. But as the kingdom expanded, he became more powerful, and with power came pride.

He no longer rose before the sun.

He no longer looked beyond the sky.

He no longer listened to the wind.

Soon there came one of the traditional days of celebration when all the people of the Southern Kingdom came to the City of Palms. They gathered before the Special Place and offered thousands of spotless, newborn lambs in gratitude to the one above. During this time, certain keepers chosen by Hope-Giver were carefully prepared to enter the sanctuary and light the incense.

"Why should the keepers get the privilege of lighting the incense?" asked the snake coiled in the corner of the palace room. "You are the most powerful person in this kingdom. You should hold the honor."

The king thought about these words, and when the lambs were sacrificed, he brashly pushed through the doors of the sanctuary and let them shut tightly behind him. An old familiar wind swept about his body as he stood in the outer chamber, stunned by its glittering beauty. But the wind was not warm, and its chill cut the king's courage.

Suddenly the doors flew open.

"What are you doing here?" demanded the chief keeper of the sanctuary.

"I am the king!"

"So you do not belong here," repeated the keeper. "You are chosen to rule, not to light the incense. You are not chosen for that, and you will not be chosen."

The king stared at the keeper and his assistants with hatred in his eyes, but he did not speak.

"Leave now," demanded the keeper. "If you do not, the hand of the one above all will humble you."

"You do not have the right to order me about," raged the king.

"These words are not mine. They belong to the one beyond the sky. You know his rights."

The king knew he had gone beyond his position, but now his honor and respect and authority before the people seemed to be at stake. So he blustered on.

"This is my kingdom and my city. Do you refuse to submit to my rule?"

The king pushed the chief keeper aside and leaned forward to light the incense.

Something unseen brushed his forehead.

It left him with a feeling of utter dread.

He felt the color drain from his face.

The chief keeper and his assistants stared at the king in horror. They hurriedly stepped back, not for fear of what the king might do, but because of the ashen mark that shone upon his brow.

The golden incense lighter dropped to the floor. The king's hands rushed to cover his face. Without seeing his reflection, he knew somehow what had been done.

"Noooo!" came his heart-wrenching cry, which silenced all who stood before the sanctuary. "Oh, help me. Oh, somebody help me."

He could see the reality in the wide-eyed stare of the chief keeper. He had the disease—the most dreaded of all diseases. The disease that meant rejection and alienation and isolation. His very presence in this place was now the worst sort of defilement. Assistants to the keeper hurriedly threw a veil over his head and helped him through the great doors and out into the sunlight. His head was bent as he shoved frantically through the crowd and out the city's gate. He ran south for a day, too humiliated to look into the face of a stranger or speak to the heart of a friend.

He did not stop until he reached the Valley of Apples. There he rested in the shade of the ancient orchards and drank from the sweet waters of a lazy brook and ate the purple fruit of the carefully kept vineyards.

The king looked beyond the sky and cried out to the one who holds stars in his hands.

"I have been so foolish. Rather than leaning upon you, I have leaned upon myself. My power made me proud, and now your hand has made me humble."

"I have always wished what was best for you," whispered the wind. "I would have spoken to you to warn you, but you have been walking far from me. Your ears were tuned to other voices."

"Today I shall return to your ways and listen to your words, whatever your judgment," said the king. "If I am worthy of your mercy, please lift this disease from my face."

"I know my words are difficult," whispered the wind with a soft compassion. "From this day forward you shall be known as Leper King, and you shall rule from this valley. You shall never again sleep in your palace or walk in your city or eat with your family."

The king's heart broke at what he heard, and tears flowed freely from his eyes.

"But I shall not leave you," continued the wind. "Together we shall walk the valley like Man walked the Garden so long ago.

"We shall talk

"and laugh

"and share our dreams.

"I shall be Comfort-Giver to you and to the people of the Southern Kingdom and to all who walk with me."

Leper King sat in the soft grass at the edge of the brook and cooled his hot feet in the stream. The sun sparkled on the water, and the smell of fresh mint drifted on the breeze. The king scooped up a handful of soil from the water's edge and rubbed it between his palms. Such was his disease that already he did not feel the soil as easily as before.

"I have always wanted to be a farmer."

"A farmer you shall be," whistled the wind.

"And though all my friends shall turn from me, and my body shall lose its senses, you will be my comfort," said Leper King.

So the king remained in the Valley of Apples all the days of his life, each morning walking with the one beyond the sky. And his son sat on the golden throne in the magnificent City of Palms.

TO SEE THE SHAPE
OF ETERNITY
OPENS THE EYES
TO EVERYDAY VISION.

CHAPTER 2
THE WRITER

H is land is a vineyard on a fertile hillside." Writer sat in the center of
the City of Palms and read aloud the words that had been carefully written
on the large sheepskin scroll. He was a young man with a quick mind and
strong voice. A crowd gathered as he read his parable.

"He dug the soil

"and removed the stones

"and planted the choicest vines.

"He tilled the ground and pruned the plants and pulled the briars. He
built a watchtower and a wall and a winepress. He did all that could be
done to produce good wine.

"But the crop was a great disappointment. Some grapes were sour and
some were shriveled and some were stunted in their immaturity. The maker
of the vineyard walked through each row with his head bent in sorrow.

" 'When a vineyard produces bad fruit,' said the maker, 'what is its owner
to do?' "

Writer looked up from his scroll into the faces of those gathered about him.
No one responded.

"I will tell you what the owner is going to do with his vineyard: He will
break down its walls and uproot its plants and let the briars overtake its rows."

"Why are you telling us this story?" asked a respected merchant.

"What does it mean?" responded another.

Writer rolled the scroll and stood to his feet. "Comfort-Giver is the owner,"
said the young man with a resonance that made the crowd uneasy. "And the

People of the Promise are the vineyard."

"You are making threats against our nation!" yelled the merchant, quickly comprehending the storyteller's meaning.

"Troublemaker!" shouted others in the crowd as they picked up stones and moved angrily toward Writer.

"These words are not mine," said the young man, looking warily for a way to escape. "These are the words of the one beyond the sky."

But the crowd grew loud and agitated. A stone flew and then another. Writer clutched his scroll and turned his back and ran away from the crowd and out the city gate. He ran south until his legs grew weak and the sun left the sky. Exhausted, he fell upon an empty field in the Valley of Apples.

An old man with a deformed face looked up as he slowly worked the sandy soil. He leaned on his hoe and shouted, "Stay away; I am Leper King. Protect yourself and flee."

The young man lifted his head and looked toward Leper King, but he did not flee.

"Did you hear my warning?" asked the king.

"Yes," said Writer with no sign of concern. "And I have often stood in your presence in the palace when I was younger, for I am a child of the keepers of the Special Place. I have always wished to speak with you. You have ruled the Southern Kingdom for over fifty summers and have walked far with the one who holds stars in his hands."

"It has been a long life and my leaving is near," said Leper King. "My body aches and is feeble and has lost much of its feeling. I can hardly use my hands and feet anymore. My memory fades or I would remember you. Soon I shall walk beyond the Blue Planet and smell the sweet soil of eternity."

"Before you go," said Writer, "may I write your story so all will learn the lessons of love and the dangers of pride?"

So Writer took up a hoe and worked beside the king. While they turned the soil together, he heard the stories of the kingdom and of the old man's walks before the dawn. Each night he picked up his stylus and wrote what he had heard.

The two talked as they planted;

and laughed as they carried life-giving water to the seedlings;

and shared their love for the one who brings the harvest.

Late one night at the end of the growing season, a servant knocked on the door of the hut Writer had rented from a local farmer.

"Leper King has left us," said the servant.

Writer bent his head and caught his breath. "He was a grand king and a good person," said the young man with a catch in his throat and a tear in his eye.

The following day the body of Leper King was buried in a field near the royal tombs of the City of Palms. Because of his disease, his form could not lay beside his father and the great kings of the Shepherd Dynasty. But Writer looked at the simple field of burial and smiled. Leper King loved the soil, and it was right that his body should rest deep within its arms.

Before the moon finished its next cycle, Writer went to the palace with a thick scroll bound to his back. He stood patiently and respectfully before Leper's son. The king had held the throne while his father lived in the Valley of Apples, but now the crown was fully his own. The son loved his father and followed the ways of the one who holds stars in his hands.

"I have heard of you," said Leper's son. "I have heard how you were chased from this city and how you befriended my father in his isolation."

"Yes," said Writer, "and I stand before you to give you his story." The young man handed the scroll to the king. "Here are the words and wisdom of your father."

The king took the scroll and held it tight. "Let me do something for you. I command that this city welcome you as a friend. From this day forward, you shall have the protection of the throne and the freedom to speak the words of Comfort-Giver."

That twilight, as the sun touched the edge of the Blue Planet and a handful of faint stars marked the beginning of night, Writer went to the sanctuary. With his father he sacrificed a spotless, newborn lamb and watched the smoke blend with the blackness. He was himself a keeper of one of the noble families of the city and one of those chosen to enter the doors into the outer chamber of the Special Place, where Leper King had dared to go unbidden. The room shimmered in the warm glow of the golden candles.

Amazing images of angels danced across the walls in the flickering flames.

Suddenly the room shone brighter.

The angels danced faster.

The flutter of wings beat louder.

The sanctuary spun recklessly and then exploded into a blinding brilliance. Writer fell to the floor and covered his eyes with both hands in fear. He removed his hands and saw that the roof now reached up and up and out, beyond even the sky. Before him was a golden throne with feet on the floor, but a back that faded into the black of night. The throne was embedded with a thousand sparkling jewels that shimmered like the stars.

A wind stirred the outer chamber and the blurry outline of a translucent robe stretched from the mighty throne and filled the room with its fabric. Writer found in horror that he lay on the shining robe, but there was nowhere to stand where he might not soil it. The flutter of wings drew his face upward. The angels now encircled the throne, announcing the glory and grandeur and awesomeness of the one above all.

The throne blazed with heat and light. The sanctuary shook, and smoke filled the room.

"I must die," cried Writer. "I have seen the shape of the one above all. If the king's presence in the sanctuary made him a leper, my coming to this place is far more unworthy."

Without looking up, he felt the air stirred by rustling angel wings above him.

"Why must you die?" asked the angels.

"Because Comfort-Giver is infinite and eternal and all-powerful, while I am one of the broken ones. Comfort-Giver told me the story of the vineyard. I know that I am part of the nation he must tear down."

"Then this is the place you must be," said the angel as he flew to the altar on which a fire of sacrifice roared. He took long metal tongs and reached into the very center of the flames and pulled out a blazing ember.

In a moment he returned and touched Writer's face with the coal. There was a brilliant searing flash. It was as if a shell had been burned away from about Writer's soul—everything felt new and clean and exhilarating. He rubbed his eyes and looked into the face of the angel.

"Your brokenness is gone," said the angel. "Your words shall now be clear and smooth and strong as you speak to those who walk the Blue Planet."

The sanctuary shook again and even more smoke filled the room. A thunderous voice boomed from far above.

"Whom shall I send?"

Writer raised his head.

He extended his hand toward the sound above.

"If you wish to send someone, I am here. Send me wherever you wish, and I will go."

"Go to the people of your kingdom," said the great voice. "Tell them of the promise of the rainbow, that I am always close and I will always care."

"I will speak your words to every person in the Southern Kingdom."

"I know you are willing. But you must know that the people to whom you speak will not listen. Like the merchants in the city who answered your words with rocks, most have been drawn away by Shining One. Their hearts are hard and their eyes are dim and their ears are dull. I ask you to go to a people who will hate your voice."

"Then how long shall I try?"

"Until the cities fall and the fields burn and the people are scattered."

Suddenly the room was dark and the voice was silent. Writer stood to his feet and sniffed a trace of sulfur in the air. He walked into the night but still heard the flutter of wings in the distance. The city was asleep, but Writer went directly to the palace.

He knocked hard on the door and, when a guard answered, he said, "May I speak to the king?"

Moments later Writer was telling Leper's son all that he had seen and heard and done.

"I know that what you say is true," said the king, "for I can still see the glow upon your face."

The king bent before his guest and kissed his feet.

"You have seen the shape of Comfort-Giver," said the king. "I long to be as close to him as my father was. What can I do?"

"Look beyond the sky and listen to his words and walk in his ways."

"Even if I am the only one in the Southern Kingdom to do so, I will look and listen and walk all the days that I have left."

So the king fought battles and conquered enemies. In time he grew more powerful than his father. He built towns and forts and towers. He was successful in every way. All this came about because he walked daily with the one who holds the stars in his hands.

Writer smiled, for at least there was one in all the Southern Kingdom who was not distracted by Shining One.

EVIL CAN NEVER BE GOOD,
NO MATTER WHO DOES IT
OR WHY.

CHAPTER 3

THE FIRE KING

No one listens to me," said Writer.

"That is what Comfort-Giver said would happen," replied the king.

"I expected that the people would not hear," said Writer, "but your son is the worst. He clings to the words and ways of the ancient snake, while he mocks the maker of all."

"He is young and immature," said the grieving father. "Give him some time. Soon he will realize his foolishness and face the truth."

"You do not see your son through clear eyes. His heart is full of anger and rebellion and anarchy."

"He is my firstborn son, and I shall allow no one to speak against him," said the king with a firm voice.

"But what if I speak the words of Comfort-Giver?"

"My son is my son."

"What about your own command," said Writer, "that I would have the protection of the throne to speak the words of Comfort-Giver?"

The king bent his head and walked away without giving an answer.

Writer went to the streets of the city and once more shouted to the crowds as they rushed about in their daily routines of busyness.

"Woe to those who seek only pleasure.

"Woe to those who call evil good and who say that good is evil.

"Woe to those who are wise in their own eyes."

No one stopped and no one listened and no one cared about Writer's words.

As the summers passed, Writer continually confronted the crowds. The king supported the truth teller in all he said, but he closed his mind to the understanding that each woe given by Writer was best illustrated by his wayward eldest son.

When the king left his life to go to Comfort-Giver's house, his son took the throne and was crowned as heir to his father's kingdom. But the son had not come to realize his foolishness nor did he face the truth. The new king believed the promises of Shining One and was held tightly in the snake's grasp.

"Whatever you wish I will provide," said the snake.

"I wish wealth—giant mounds of silver and gold—enough to fill my royal palace."

"If you wish wealth, so be it," said the snake. "But there is one thing you must do to show your faithfulness to my ways."

"Whatever you ask, I will do."

"Go to the valley west of the city and chop down a hundred trees. Stack the wood large and tall into a mighty fire that will send sparks high above the Blue Planet."

"Why should I build such a fire?" asked the king.

"Because it will get you what you want," said the serpent. "Once the flames are hot and raging, gather your sons. One at a time throw them into the fire."

The king was silent, but he understood. Those who followed the serpent had long shown their devotion by casting their first children alive into a flaming fire of sacrifice. His father had wiped out the sacrifices. Now they would once again begin, and the king would show before all the nation that his love for the snake was greatest of all.

"What you order is a difficult thing," he whispered with a shudder. "How can I kill all my sons, whom I love?"

"Because you love wealth more. You will give me your children."

The next day the king went to the evil valley where the serpent had been worshiped in days gone by. He built the pyre and threw his sons into its flames. The boys screamed and the people cheered and Writer wept. The serpent smiled as he slipped silently into the midst of the blaze. From that day on, this place was known as the Valley of Flames, and the new leader was Fire King. His royal palace was filled with giant mounds of silver and gold.

Far to the east, in the shadows of the Mountains of the Dawn, the Kingdom of the Bull snorted and stamped its hoof. A handful of nations formed an alliance to stand against this bloodthirsty foe, but Fire King refused to join.

"Why would I wish to join your foolish little plot?" shouted Fire King. "We have an agreement with the Kingdom of the Bull. Besides, the Southern Kingdom is as strong as it has ever been, and Shining One has given me all the wealth my palace can hold."

"But if you join us, we will have more power to resist the army of our enemy," said the delegation.

"But you would still be weak and pitiful and poor. Go home and hide in your huts with your women." On his signal, the king's fully armed warriors surrounded the alliance delegation and removed them from the City of Palms. They went away to their respective lands, full of hatred for the Southern Kingdom and its obstinate king. The following spring, the alliance invaded the Southern Kingdom. The alliance army took land and burned fields and shattered cities. They attacked the City of Palms. The capital stood strong, though as the battle cries echoed about the well-built walls, the Southern Kingdom saw heavy losses.

Mighty warriors fell.

Women and children were captured.

A great deal of plunder was gathered.

After a few months, the alliance army turned its back on the city and went its own way. A year later they returned, however. Runners came to Fire King with word that a massive army camped in the hill country north of his city. As the king heard this report, his heart shook like it had never shook before. That night he left the palace by torchlight and went to the bubbling spring east of the city. He drank deep from the pure water but could not calm himself.

"Do not be afraid."

Fire King fumbled for his sword and swung around to face the voice.

Writer was standing in the shadows. He had not been welcome in the palace since Fire King had been crowned. The king had almost put him out of his mind, but now he craved his words.

"Look up to the stars," Writer continued.

The king looked, his hands trembling.

"These are reminders of a new promise Comfort-Giver has for his people: No matter how dark the path, he will always show the way."

"But I have taunted my enemies. Now they come to destroy me."

"This is not the time for your city to fall," said Writer. "Turn to the one beyond the sky and he will comfort you."

"I will never look beyond the sky," said Fire King as his fear turned to stubborn anger.

"If you look to him, he will give you wisdom and guide you to victory."

"I have given my children to Shining One. He shall be my victory. I will go to the witches and wizards and those who speak to the dead. But I will never look to Comfort-Giver."

So Fire King went to those who bow to Shining One. They told him to seek assistance from the Kingdom of the Bull.

"Please don't," begged Writer. "That kingdom is a worse enemy than the alliance."

"You are not my counselor," the man on the throne said with an angry growl. "I am king. I will seek help from wherever and from whomever I wish."

The next day the armies of the Northern King and the Caravan King surrounded the City of Palms.

They pounded the walls

and stormed the gates

and cut off the city from outside help.

The people within wept, but Fire King refused to look beyond the sky. Instead he sent a runner through the secret tunnels that led outside the city walls, with a royal scroll for the King of the Bull.

"I have paid to you all the tribute you have asked. Now my kingdom is under siege. Be my protector and I will reward you richly."

Bull King agreed to help. His army was ready to go to war quickly. He attacked the City of Caravans, captured its people, and killed its king. The army continued south until he had taken all the mountains and valleys and rivers of the Northern Kingdom except the City on the Hill. By then the siege had been lifted at the City of Palms, and the armies fled to protect their own lands. Fire King stripped the wealth and beauty from the sanctuary; he took the giant mounds of silver and gold from the royal palace; he demanded wealth from the people. All that he had desired so much was delivered to the Kingdom of the Bull.

Fire King went to the City of Caravans to meet with Bull King.

"Let us go to the altar of Shining One," said Bull King, "and sacrifice to the master of anarchy."

So the two kings stood before the most beautiful altar Fire King had ever seen. They sacrificed a thousand animals of every kind. Fire King was so impressed by this altar that he had detailed drawings of it sketched and sent to the chief keeper of the sanctuary.

"Make this altar for me and spare no expense. Make it big and bright and beautiful. Set it in the most prominent place before the doors of the sanctuary, where the large copper altar to Comfort-Giver now stands."

Fire King was well pleased with his golden altar. He sacrificed a spotless, newborn lamb to Shining One on his new altar, and he commanded all the city to sacrifice only on this altar. The altar to Comfort-Giver that had been made by the craftsmen of Wise King so many summers ago was hidden in the shadows and forgotten by all but those who remained faithful.

A short time later, Bull King announced a visit to the City of Palms. In preparation for his arrival, Fire King destroyed every item left within the sanctuary except the ark of mystery, which even he was afraid to touch. Then he locked its doors and boarded up its entrance. The people looked on in shock. Though few looked beyond the sky, the closing of the Special Place seemed desperately wrong. Now serpentine statues were carefully crafted and placed in the plazas where people gathered.

"Why do you follow the wicked ways of the Bull King? Why do you try to impress one who is full of anarchy?" shouted Writer on the steps of the palace. "The kingdom you admire so much soon will die."

"The Kingdom of the Bull is the greatest nation the Blue Planet has known," said the king. "They are invincible. Such a great and rich and powerful nation will never die."

"Comfort-Giver saved them when Reluctant Prophet spoke boldly some thirty summers ago in the City of Blood. But they no longer remember his words. So now Comfort-Giver says:

" 'I shall remove their boundaries

" 'and plunder their treasure

" 'and bring down their mighty men.' "

"If it was not for my father's command of royal protection, I would have you cut down on this spot."

"Beware," said Writer, "for the future looks much darker than the past. Sooner than you can see, the dragon shall swallow the bull and then the dragon shall swallow all that we know."

Fire King was enraged.

He shook in his fury.

He cursed the words he feared were true.

CHAPTER 4

THE COMMITTED KING

He was deeply troubled by the actions of Fire King. What most frightened him was that he was Fire King's oldest son. Had he been born second or third, he would have joined his brothers in the flames of the great fire in the evil valley. As it was, he would one day be king, and what kind of kingdom was to be his inheritance? Why was his father's heart so hardened against the one who holds stars in his hands? Why would a king lock the doors to Comfort-Giver's sanctuary? But then how could a father throw his sons into the flames?

As the summers passed, the son watched his father's foolishness and grew wise. He saw how Fire King was deceived by the lies of Shining One and how stubbornly he refused to face truth.

In frustration, the son wandered the streets one night, lost in thought.

"You come from a mighty dynasty," came a strong voice.

A middle-aged man stood alone in the lonely plaza, illuminated only by the full moon above. The form in the darkness looked vaguely familiar.

"You are of the line of Shepherd King," said Writer. "I knew your grandfather. I wrote the story of your great-grandfather. Both men were wise and true and good."

"But my father?"

"He followed a path of dishonor and death and destruction."

"Can I regain the truth?" The son looked earnestly into the eyes of Writer.

"Rise before the light touches the Mountains of the Dawn and walk humbly with the maker of all.

"Look beyond the sky.

"Call upon his name.

"Listen to the voice of the wind."

"I will try to commit my whole heart to the words and ways of Comfort-Giver."

The committed one tried to speak to his father of these things, but Fire King became angry and threatened to take his breath if the name of the one who holds stars was ever mentioned in his presence again.

Meanwhile the Blue Planet was in turmoil. Bull King sent his forces against the Northern Kingdom and besieged the City on the Hill. After three hard years the city fell. Its people were taken to a faraway place at the foot of the Mountains of the Dawn.

Several summers later, Fire King swore at the sky and gripped his throne and breathed his final breath. His son closed the king's eyes and kissed his cheek.

"Oh, Father, if only you had accepted the truth, your heart would have known peace."

The son was crowned as the Committed King. He unlocked the doors of the sanctuary and returned the copper altar to its proper place. He restored the Special Place and destroyed the serpentine statues.

"Every morning I walk with Comfort-Giver," said the king, "but I wish to walk closer to the one who holds stars in his hands."

"Read the ancient scrolls," said Writer.

So Committed King read the ancient scrolls about the Garden and the Builder and the General. He studied the history of his people and the faithfulness of Comfort-Giver. The stories opened his eyes and deepened his devotion. So the king called all the people of the Southern Kingdom to gather before the sanctuary. He pleaded with them to put aside the wickedness of Shining One. He asked them to humble their hearts and sacrifice a lamb and gave thanks to the one above all. And many were ready to do so. The city celebrated. For seven days the people feasted and sang and looked beyond the sky. Not since the days of Wise King had such joy filled the land.

"Shall we continue our friendship with the Kingdom of the Bull?"

Committed King asked the wind.

"Do not serve them or envy them or befriend them," said the wind.

"But if we do not, they will attack us."

"The City of Palms will not fall to the forces of the bull."

Committed King did as Comfort-Giver said and prepared for an attack. He reinforced the city wall.

He built a second wall around the first.

He erected sturdy watchtowers to watch for invaders.

Then he supplied a mighty army with spears and swords and shields. He had many summers to do all this before the Kingdom of the Bull made its move against the fortified cities of the Southern Kingdom.

"Be strong and courageous," said Committed King. "Comfort-Giver is our victory. Bull King and his vast army cannot stand against the one above all."

The people of the city and the warriors of the land cheered at the king's words. They looked beyond the sky and their confidence grew, until the Army of the Bull approached. Then even Committed King hesitated.

"Are you sure you are doing what is right?" hissed the ancient serpent. "Comfort-Giver said not to befriend your enemy, but did he say not to talk to them or negotiate with them or give them your silver and gold?"

"Possibly that could save the City of Palms," said the king.

"You are the leader," said the snake, "and you should take action before it is too late."

The king listened seriously to these words. He sent a runner with a royal scroll to the Bull King.

"I should not have resisted a kingdom as powerful as yours," read the runner from the royal scroll. "Withdraw from my borders, and I will pay whatever you demand."

"Tell your master that I demand eleven wagons of silver and a single wagon of gold."

Committed King emptied the palace treasury and stripped the sacred sanctuary. He sent all the silver and gold that had been demanded.

Bull King laughed when he saw the twelve wagons, heavy with tribute, moving toward him. Then he sent his highest commander with a large portion of his army to the City of Palms. The field officer walked to the wall and called out to the people: "Do not listen to Committed King. He cannot deliver you from the Kingdom of the Bull.

"Make peace with us.

"Open wide your gates.

"Let us take you away to a much better land.

"Your new home will be full of rich harvests and plump vineyards and sweet honey. Choose life, not death. Comfort-Giver has turned his back on you. Do not listen to Committed King."

The people of the city remained silent and said nothing.

Committed King went to the Special Place and bent his head to the one who holds stars in his hands.

The king's officers stood nearby.

"Writer has sent a message from Comfort-Giver," said one of the officers. "It says, 'Do not be afraid, for the enemy's words are empty. Go to your watchtower and see the Bull Army retreat.' "

So Committed King went to his watchtower and looked down on the enemy that stood before his gates. He watched as runners came from the west. The commander received the runners and soon the field officers were summoned. They sat in a circle in the open camp, talking with great intensity. As the king watched, the meeting broke up and horns sounded. By late afternoon the warriors had broken camp and were withdrawing from the City of Palms.

As the enemy marched away, a message arrived from the enemy commander: "Do not be deceived. We shall return. And when we do, not even Comfort-Giver can save you."

Committed King shook his head at the arrogance of such words. He went to the sanctuary and fell to his knees and looked beyond the sky.

"The Kingdom of the Bull does not understand that you are the maker of all. Deliver us from the bull. Break the back of this army and send it home without victory so that every kingdom on the Blue Planet will know that you are infinite and eternal and all-powerful."

That night a shadow crossed the moon. The angel of death visited the vast Army of the Bull. With his flaming sword, he silently struck a fatal blow while the camp slept securely in delusions of its invincibility. As the sun awoke the morning, cries of shock and terror and grief echoed across the hills. The back of the army was broken with more than half of its warriors dead.

Bull King wept as he looked into the eyes of what was left of his once-mighty army. Within a cycle of the moon, he was back in the City of Blood. There in the temple of Shining One he bowed before a golden statue of the snake and cried out, "Where is our victory? Where is your power? Where is. . . ?" His prayer was interrupted by a sword thrust into his back and through his heart. He turned as he fell to look into the eyes of his own sons.

At the same time in the City of Palms, Committed King became ill.

His face was pale.

His strength was gone.

His life balanced on the point of death.

Writer came to the king and stood beside his bed and took the sick man's hand. "Your heart has grown proud and your commitment has wavered. You gave silver and gold to the Kingdom of the Bull rather than trusting in the strength of Comfort-Giver. Therefore put your house in order, because you are about to die."

Writer let go of the feeble hand and left the room.

Committed King wept, not because of his passing, but because of his failure to trust.

"Forgive my failures," he cried. "Most of my life I have walked with you and listened to your words and done all that you asked. Give me one more chance to show you that I am fully committed to the one who holds stars in his hands."

As Writer was leaving the city, the wind whispered to him. "Return to the king. Tell him that I have heard his words and seen his tears. I will add fifteen summers to his life."

Writer returned to the king with these words. Soon Committed King left his bed and went to the sanctuary and sacrificed a spotless, newborn lamb to the giver of all comfort.

Not long afterward, a royal caravan arrived from far to the east.

"I am the son of the Dragon King," said a young man dressed in the finest cloth Committed King had ever seen. "My father sent me, bearing gifts. He heard of your illness, and wishes you good health."

"The illness is gone," said the king. "My body is strong, for Comfort-Giver can heal the deepest disease and bring comfort to the greatest pain."

The son of the Dragon King gave many gifts. Committed King escorted the royal caravan through the City of Palms. He showed them the ornate palace and double walls and sturdy watchtowers. He took them to the Special Place and the treasury and the many storehouses.

"You have a wonderful city and a blessed kingdom," said Dragon King's son. "We can be friends and work together. We have a wicked enemy, the Kingdom of the Bull. But maybe if we stand side by side, we can protect both our kingdoms."

Committed King agreed.

After the caravan left the city, Writer approached the king. "Where did the caravan come from? What did they want?"

"The royal son came from the City of Stars, capital of the Kingdom of the Dragon. They came to befriend us, and I have shown them our greatness so that we might work together as equals."

"How could you do such a thing?" Writer hit the wall in a sudden burst of anger that astounded the king.

"What is wrong?"

"The man you have just met will one day rule the world, and you have shown him the secrets of this city and the reasons he should bother conquering you."

"How could I have known?"

"You should have asked Comfort-Giver for discernment. You should have remembered the recorded words I told your father many summers ago: 'Sooner than you can see, the Dragon shall swallow the Bull and then the Dragon shall swallow all that we know.' "

SMALL CHOICES
SHAPE THE FUTURE
AND SOMETIMES SHAKE
ALL WITHIN ONE'S GRASP.

Chapter 5

THE UNCOMMITTED KINGS

Y ou are now the king," said the snake. "You can do whatever you wish."

"But I do not know how to be king," said the young, scrawny man who sat uneasily on the golden throne.

"Listen to me, and I will lead you to greatness beyond your dreams."

So the new king listened to the snake and did all that he said.

He built altars to the golden calf.

He shaped statues to the serpent.

He bowed before the stars.

"These are not the ways of your father," said a crowd of people who gathered before the royal palace to speak with the new king.

"I am not my father," said the king. "I have found another way to stand against our enemies."

"But how can there be a better way than the way of Comfort-Giver?" someone in the crowd asked.

"There are secrets that not even the one beyond the sky can fathom," said the king.

"That is not true," said the keepers of the Special Place. "Comfort-Giver is infinite and eternal and all-powerful."

"Do you challenge my words?" demanded the king.

"We stand by the truth known by your father."

"My father is dead. I have chosen a different path. I will not allow anyone to question my direction."

He had been born after the death of his grandfather, the Fire King, but there was something in the stories of Fire King's majestic defiance against Comfort-Giver that seemed heroic to the impressionable young man. In the dark of the night, he slipped beyond the city walls to meet with witches and wizards and those who spoke to the dead. Some of them had counseled his grandfather and had been in hiding during the reign of Committed King.

"I want to speak to my grandfather," he said in the shadows.

"Then light the fires in the Valley of Flames," croaked a haggard, old witch. "Throw your sons into the heat and your grandfather shall appear."

So the king ordered the great bonfires lit and he escorted his two boy children out of the palace.

"No!" demanded the keepers of the Special Place as they blocked the king's path. "This is wrong. You shall not throw your sons into the fire."

"Get out of my way before I lose my patience," said the king.

"Only if you turn from the Valley of Flames," said the keepers.

"No one tells me what to do!" shouted the king. "Guards! Kill them!"

Swords flashed and keepers fell and blood flowed.

The king continued on his way to the Valley of Flames. Many followers of Shining One circled the giant bonfire and cheered the king as he stood near the raging inferno. He motioned his sons forward, and sweat rolled down their foreheads. He placed his hands on their shoulders and the people chanted. With a violent thrust, the king shoved his two small boys into the center of the heat.

The young screams were quickly swallowed by the crackling of the fire. The king watched his sons die, and as he stared into the blaze, he saw his grandfather dancing among the flames.

The king turned toward the crowd and raised his hands high above his head. The people clapped and danced wildly and shouted in delight.

The king felt triumph.

The snake sizzled in delight.

And Writer screamed.

Everybody looked toward the massive walls of the City of Palms. There standing tall atop the stone battlements was the old graybeard.

"What evil have you done?" The words echoed loud and clear across the valley.

"I am king and I may do whatever I choose."

"The one above all looks down on this valley and weeps," shouted Writer. "If you choose evil over good, he will remove his hand of protection from your city. The Kingdom of the Bull waits at your border, hungry and restless and ready to swallow your nation. The Northern Kingdom tried Comfort-Giver's patience, and the bull plundered their capital. Now the Southern Kingdom does the same. Do you think you can avoid your fate?"

"Shining One is my protector," said the king, "and he will lead me to greatness."

"He shall lead you to destruction."

"Silence!"

"Even your grandfather allowed me the freedom to speak the words of Comfort-Giver."

"But with me those words shall end," declared the king.

"The words of Comfort-Giver shall never end," said Writer.

"Kill him!" called the king to his soldiers. "Do not let him leave this kingdom alive."

The soldiers searched for Writer in a forest near the city walls. Here the man of truth hid in a hollowed-out tree, but the captain of the soldiers saw movement in the rotten trunk. His men brought a large saw. Back and forth, the teeth cut into the tree.

Writer whispered to the wind. "I am ready to walk with you beyond the sky."

"Come to me," said the wind, "and your comfort shall be complete."

Back and forth, the saw severed the tree and the man.

The king looked at what he had done, and for a moment he wondered whether he had gone too far. He wondered at the words of Comfort-Giver and if Shining One was truly as mighty as he claimed. But the time was now past for such questioning. He had already chosen the way of his allegiance.

Soon many thousands of warriors from the Kingdom of the Bull invaded the Southern Kingdom. They looted and plundered the land. They invaded the City of Palms and captured the king.

A metal hook was placed in his nose.

Bronze shackles bound his hands and feet.

A heavy weight was strapped to his bent back.

"Shining One, please help me," cried out the king.

But there was no answer.

The king was taken beyond the Great River. He was beaten and tortured and humiliated. As he sat alone in a dark and dirty dungeon, he remembered the words of Writer and the deeds of his committed father. He regretted the altars he had built and the fires he had burned and the blood he had spilled.

The king humbled his heart and cried to the one he had always rejected. "Help me to be like my father," he wept as he committed his whole heart to the words and ways of Comfort-Giver.

A few days later the king was released from his shackles and his dungeon. The King of the Bull allowed him to return to the City of Palms. As soon as he reached his gates, he ordered that the altars to the golden calf be torn down. He shattered the statues to the serpent. He assigned new keepers to the Special Place and sacrificed spotless, newborn lambs on the altar before the sanctuary. Soon all those in the Southern Kingdom looked beyond the sky.

The king grew strong and prosperous and reigned longer than any other king of the new land. When he died, his oldest son wore the crown. But the son had learned none of the lessons of his father, and he was a cruel and inept king who was hated immediately by all within the kingdom.

He built altars to the golden calf.

He shaped statues to the serpent.

He bowed before the stars.

Hated King did everything his father did before he was humbled, but he did it with more vengeance and ambition. His heart was hard to Comfort-Giver, and he cursed the memory of his father for turning to the one who holds stars in his hands.

"Anyone who looks to Comfort-Giver must die!" shouted the Hated King.

Many people clung to the one above all, but they feared for their lives. "We must kill this king before he kills us," some whispered to the keepers of the Special Place.

"No," said the keepers. "The king is an evil man full of hatred and violence and anarchy, but he is still our king. Do not do him any harm. Be patient and let Comfort-Giver grant our king his due."

"But what if he steals our wives and throws our sons into the flames?"

"We must rest in the one above all," said the keepers, "and let him comfort our fears."

The people returned to their homes and trusted Comfort-Giver with their lives. But their hatred of the king continued to grow.

After two summers, the hatred was so intense that the king's advisors feared that a rebellion was about to begin. Still, the king was stubborn.

"I do not care if they hate me," he ranted. "I am king and I can do whatever I wish."

He built giant bonfires bigger than had ever been seen in the Valley of Flames.

"Bring me the sons of the city," he shouted from his throne, "and let me throw them into the fire."

The advisors were aghast at such a command. They huddled in the hall outside the throne room and spoke of the king.

"He has gone mad."

"He is destroying our kingdom."

"He must be killed."

So the advisors asked to speak to the king in private. The king dismissed his guards. While some of the advisors talked to him, others crept into the evening shadows of the throne room.

As the Hated King became absorbed in the discussion, the hidden advisors burst from the shadows, clutching daggers in their hands. They approached the king from behind. One grabbed his hair and pulled his head back. The other slashed his dagger across the exposed neck.

Hated King struggled and shuddered and went limp as blood soaked his royal robe. The advisors took the body to the steps of the palace and cried out to the city:

"We are free."

"We have nothing to fear."

"Our sons have been saved."

"What you have done is wrong," said the keepers of the Special Place. "You were told to be patient and let Comfort-Giver grant our king his due."

"But our king was so evil that he would have thrown all our sons into the fire."

"Comfort-Giver is our protector. He would have dealt with the king. Instead he must deal with you."

"But the king was hated by all."

"Guards!" called the chief keeper. "Arrest these men!"

Guards grabbed the advisors and took them outside the city gate. There they were thrown down an embankment, and the crowd picked up stones and killed all who had been involved in the plot to assassinate the king.

The City of Palms humbled its heart and looked beyond the sky and asked, "What shall we do now?"

A sweet wind blew through the streets with a whisper that could only be heard by those with hearts that were fully open.

"Follow me."

TRUTH IS A CHERISHED LIGHT
FOR THOSE WHO STAND
IN THE VALLEY OF SHADOWS.

CHAPTER 6

THE BOOK KING

H e cannot be king," said the keepers among themselves. "He is only eight summers old."

"But he is Hated King's oldest living son," said the chief keeper.

"His father was so evil he would have taken our children into the Valley of Flames."

"For 350 summers we have been led by the line of Shepherd. Comfort-Giver established this dynasty, and we cannot tamper with it. Instead we will surround the king and lead him into the ways of truth and point his face beyond the sky."

So the people crowned the young king, and the keepers of the sanctuary raised him. When he reached his sixteenth birthday, the king sat in the royal courtyard. A strong hot breeze caused the palm trees to shudder and the water of the shallow pool to ripple.

"Be silent before your maker," said the wind.

The king bowed his head and let the wind wash over him.

"Your city does not listen to my words or respect my ways or walk with me."

"I will walk with you," whispered the king without raising his head. "I will follow where you lead."

From that day forward, he rose before the sun touched the Mountains of the Dawn and walked the highlands eagerly.

The longer the king walked with the one above all, the stronger the Southern Kingdom grew. The Kingdom of the Bull lost much of its power and withdrew from the new land. The young king expanded his boundaries to include much of what had once been the Northern Kingdom. It was a time of power and peace and prosperity.

As the young king walked the hills and valleys of his increased kingdom, he saw much that hurt his heart.

"Why do so many of my people follow the ways of Shining One?"

"The northern kings set wicked examples, as did your father and grandfather."

"But the people hated my father, and my grandfather changed."

"When violence and selfishness and anarchy are planted deep, they are difficult to uproot."

"I am one man, but my heart aches at what I see. I will do all I can to uproot the evil throughout the land."

So he called the people to turn from their darkness.

He tore down the altars to the golden calf.

He shattered the statues to the serpent.

He burned the temples to the Shining One.

Comfort-Giver smiled. "I am moved by your courage and determination, but there is more that must be done."

"Whatever you ask, I will do."

"The Special Place is badly in need of repair," whispered the wind.

The king immediately called the best carpenters and stonecutters and craftsmen. "Return the sanctuary to its splendor. I will provide all that is needed of stone or timber, cloth or incense, silver or gold."

The workers rebuilt and repaired and restored Comfort-Giver's sanctuary. As all within the Special Place was made new, the chief keeper found scrolls wrapped in sheepskin that had been hidden in a secret place. Carefully he unrolled his find and gasped in excitement.

Clutching the scroll, he ran to the king, who was meeting with his advisors.

"Look," he said as he gently, reverently unrolled the scroll. "It is the Book of Beginnings and the Book of Leaders."

"I thought my grandfather destroyed all the ancient scrolls before he turned to Comfort-Giver."

"A keeper must have hidden this one. He may have been killed before he could tell his secret."

"Read it to me," commanded the king.

" 'There was a time before time began when the Blue Planet was black, pitch black without a hint of light anywhere,' " started the keeper as he artfully articulated each ancient word.

The king listened with all his heart and soul and mind. The sun touched the roof of the sky and slowly dropped until it splashed below the surface of the Great Sea, but still the keeper read.

The king did not move. His eyes focused on the keeper, and his ears tuned to every inflection until the final word.

Then the keeper set down the scroll,

and the advisors looked to the king,

and the king tore his clothes.

"We have failed," wept the king as he went to the Special Place and sacrificed a spotless, newborn lamb to the one beyond the sky. Falling on the ground before the altar, he pledged his whole heart and all his ways to the ultimate source.

"Disaster will come," said the wind as it swirled about the prostrate king. "Because my people have forsaken me and continue to follow Shining One, I will crush the kingdom. But because you listened to my words and humbled your heart, I will hold back this calamity until your form sleeps peacefully beside that of your father and grandfather."

The king rose from the ground and called all the leaders of the kingdom to the city. People gathered before the Special Place. The king stood before them and raised his hand until silence spread. Then, in a voice that held authority beyond his years, he read from the lost scroll.

For the first time, the people heard the words of their history. They heard how Comfort-Giver made them and protected them and guided them to the New Land. They heard of the promise of the rainbow and the ten words from the mountain and the power of the one beyond the sky. They were amazed by all that was spoken. They gave it their full attention until the echo of the final sentence faded.

Then the people made a pledge to listen to the words of the one with stars in his hands, and follow his ways—but their pledge was more emotion than faith. Thousands of spotless, newborn lambs were sacrificed, and a sweet smoke filled the city. The people asked to hear the king read from the sacred scroll once more. From that day forward he was known as the Book King.

A young man sat outside the Special Place. He was a keeper of the sanctuary like his father before him. A breeze blew through his dark hair and he looked up.

"I have chosen you," said the wind. "I have chosen you to speak to my people."

"But I have no experience, and I do not know what to say."

"Do not be afraid, for I am with you. Go to the king and tell him you are my truth teller. Tell him that, though there is peace and prosperity today, it shall not last."

So the young man went to the royal palace and confronted Book King. "Do you remember the story of Shopkeeper and his faithless wife?"

"Yes," said the king. "Shopkeeper was like Comfort-Giver; his faithless wife was like the Northern Kingdom."

"In recent generations, the Southern Kingdom has become like the faithless wife. The one above all yearns to embrace his children with wealth and wisdom and long life, but they do not walk with him."

"They pledged to listen to his words and follow his ways," said the king.

"Their pledge has not produced practice," said the prophet. "Comfort-Giver is waiting to comfort his faithless people. If they turn toward the truth, he will spare their kingdom. But if they chase after foolishness, weeping will haunt the highlands."

The prophet and the king spoke for hours. They shared each other's concerns about the hardness of the people's hearts, and what the two of them could do to turn the kingdom toward the truth.

The young keeper of the temple walked the streets of the city, calling and pleading and weeping. The people called him the Weeping Prophet, but they did not respond.

The king rid the land of the witches and warlocks and those who spoke to the dead.

He drowned the fires of the Valley of Flames.

He opened the doors to the Special Place.

He did all that Comfort-Giver asked of him.

Still the people would not respond. Summers passed and their hearts grew harder and foolishness sealed their fate.

Toward the Mountains of the Dawn, the dragon attacked the bull. The City of Blood fell and the City of Crossroads fell. The Kingdom of the Bull was reduced to nothing but a small war-weary army in a single fortified city. In a desperate attempt to save his kingdom, Bull King sent runners across the fertile crescent to the Delta King.

"Come help us, then we will be your servants and our land will be yours. If Dragon King conquers our kingdom, he will soon threaten the Land of Pyramids."

So Delta King led a mighty army north through the New Land to rescue Bull King.

When Book King heard of these events, he gathered his forces to stop Delta King from marching through the Valley of Harvest.

"Why do you stand in my way?" asked Delta King.

"Bull King has been our enemy for many summers. They conquered our northern brothers and took them captive. We wish Dragon King to swallow what is left of the Bull, so we shall do what we can to block you from helping them."

"Comfort-Giver came to me in a dream," said Delta King. "He sent me on this mission and told me to act quickly. If you stand against me, you stand against the one above all. Lead your forces home, or Comfort-Giver will destroy you."

"You lie!" shouted Book King. "Why would Comfort-Giver send you to help my enemy?"

"I do not understand the mind of the one who holds stars in his hands, but I have heard his words."

Book King walked away in disgust, but he did not look beyond the sky, nor ask Comfort-Giver to lead him in wisdom.

"What if the words of Delta King are true?" asked Weeping Prophet. "Should we not seek the will of our maker?"

"I know his words and ways and will," said Book King in stubborn defiance. "Bull King is our enemy, and Delta King as well."

As Delta King and his army moved up the valley, Book King attacked. The Delta Army held fast.

A thousand archers stepped forward.

They pulled their bows tight.

They let their arrows fly.

The bronze-tipped shafts cut through armor and flesh. One burrowed deep into Book King's chest. Pulling back on his reins, he cried out, "Help me; I've been wounded!"

Before his warriors could gather at his side, the king had fallen. Blood soaked his clothes and ran down his shining armor. The men moved him to a chariot and raced him toward the City of Palms.

The king was weak and his voice could barely be heard. Weeping Prophet held his hand and leaned close to his mouth.

"Speak your heart, for there is little time."

"Never lean upon your own understanding," said the king. "Always seek the will of Comfort-Giver."

The prophet nodded his head as the king closed his eyes and left this life.

Weeping Prophet stood on the steps of the royal palace and cried out to the city.

"Our king was right and just.

"Our king looked beyond the sky.

"Our king was the last good king."

The people wept with the prophet as their beloved king was laid to rest.

THOSE WHO WORSHIP PUDDLES HATE THOSE WHO SPEAK OF OCEANS.

CHAPTER 7

THE PROPHET HATERS

I should be king," said the firstborn.

"But father never approved of your wild ways," said secondborn. "And I have befriended Delta King."

"How could you do such a thing?" demanded firstborn. "He killed our father and now is trying to control our kingdom."

"I will never let an outsider control our kingdom," said the thirdborn. "And I was father's favorite. If he lived, he would choose me."

"You are too young."

"You aren't dependable."

"Neither one of you know the art of leadership," said the firstborn.

The yelling increased

and threats followed

and blows fell.

"Silence!" commanded Delta King as he entered the throne room of the royal palace. "This kingdom is mine. At my word this city would be leveled."

The three sons of Book King immediately bowed low to the powerful leader of the Land of Pyramids.

"I shall choose the next king. Any who debate the issue will not live to see the sun set."

The three sons nodded in submission as they stood before Delta King. He paced before them, studying each face and staring into each set of restless eyes. Finally he stopped before the second son.

"You are my choice."

The oldest son started to protest, but with a glance, Delta King silenced him.

99

The next day the second son was crowned king of the Southern Kingdom. He sat tall on his throne and called the royal advisors before him.

"I order my brothers out of the royal palace," he began. "I want a hundred golden statues of the snake shaped and spread through the city. And gather me the best workers, for I wish to expand the palace with upper rooms and large windows and the finest cedar paneling."

From that day he was known as Cedar King, but his reign was to be a mere three cycles of the moon.

Delta King commanded Cedar King to pay tribute in gold equal to the weight of a small woman and a hundred times more in silver.

"But my kingdom cannot pay such a price," complained Cedar King.

"Throw him in chains," said Delta King to his warriors. "My commands are to be obeyed without excuse or complaint or delay. You shall be replaced."

"I am sorry," begged Cedar King as he fell to his knees. "I will collect your tribute."

"No, your older brother will take your place."

Cedar King was seized and carried away to the Land of Deltas, where he spent the rest of his days in prison.

Delta King looked into the eyes of the older brother. "How soon can you collect my silver and gold?"

"Immediately," said the new king.

So the king demanded that all the people pay silver and gold for this tribute. The people grumbled, but they gave what was asked. The new leader was known as the Tribute King.

Weeping Prophet continued to walk the streets of the City of Palms, speaking the words of Comfort-Giver. But the people bowed to the golden serpents and threatened to take the breath of the truth teller if he spoke against their evil.

"I weep for my city," the prophet cried out at the Special Place. "I see women starve in the streets and warriors fall in the field and those that are left taken into captivity. All this is about to happen because the people are hard-hearted and will not listen to the words of Comfort-Giver."

"Cease your words!" declared the keeper who kept order on the sanctuary grounds.

"I must speak the truth."

"Then arrest him," ordered the sanctuary guard, "and give him forty lashes."

Guards dragged the prophet toward the place of punishment. One, two, three times the long, leather whip left its deep red welts on his bare back. Ten, twenty, thirty.

Weeping Prophet closed his eyes
and gritted his teeth
and swayed beneath the excruciating pain.

Blood covered his back and sweat covered his face. He could not remember the last ten lashes or being thrust into the stocks at the north end of the sanctuary grounds.

The next morning he was in such pain that he was unaware of his great hunger and thirst. The chief keeper ordered the groaning man released.

"I think he has learned his lesson," said the keeper with a laugh.

Weeping Prophet looked into the keeper's eyes, weak but confident and unafraid: "You want me to be quiet, but that shall not be. This city and this kingdom will soon be handed to Dragon King, regardless of what you or the king does to me."

The keeper stared at the beaten prophet in disbelief.

"The Special Place and the palace will be plundered and burned. You and all who live in your house will be taken across the Great River, where you will die as captives in a strange land."

Other keepers were shocked at the prophet's words.

"He must be punished," said an elderly keeper who walked with a staff.

"A beating did not silence him," said another.

"Throw him into prison," said the elderly one.

"No prison will keep him quiet."

"Then he must die." The elderly one's staff slammed down onto the ground.

The other keepers agreed. As one, they seized the prophet and took him to the leaders of the kingdom.

"This man speaks disaster against our people," declared the old one. "He deserves to die."

"I speak what Comfort-Giver tells me to speak," whispered the Weeping

Prophet in his pain. "I am an innocent man, but I place myself in your hands to do with as you think right."

The leaders met for hours. Then they spoke to the keepers. "This man should not be put to death, for he has only given us the words of the maker of all."

The prophet walked free.

The keepers spat on the ground.

The king swore at the sky.

In his anger, Tribute King reignited the fires in the Valley of Flames. He bowed to the statues of the snake and gave his heart to Shining One. He ordered Weeping Prophet to never again step foot onto the grounds of the Special Place.

Across the fertile crescent on the shores of the Great River, Delta King clashed against Dragon King. The clash was mighty and decisive. The Kingdom of the Dragon chased its enemy toward the setting sun. During that winter, a wind blew through the city and spoke to Weeping Prophet. "Take a scroll and write all the words I tell you. Let the people know that there is a fiery dragon who will do great damage to their kingdom."

So the prophet called his assistant. What he dictated, his assistant wrote on the scroll.

When they were done, Weeping Prophet said to his assistant: "I am forbidden to go to the Special Place, so go and read to the people the words on this scroll."

The assistant went to the Special Place and read from the scroll. A wise man heard the words and went to the leaders of the kingdom.

"I have heard the most powerful words. You must hear them for yourselves."

The leaders sent an official to the prophet's assistant with the message: "Bring us your scroll and read it to us."

The words were indeed powerful. The leaders sat in amazement at all they heard.

"Where did you get this scroll?" they asked.

"Weeping Prophet dictated the words and I wrote them," said the assistant.

"We must show this to the king," said one of the leaders, "but he will be angry. You and the prophet must go into hiding. Do not let anyone know where you are; for if the king finds you, you will die."

The leaders took the scroll to Tribute King, who was sitting in his palace warming himself before a small fire. They showed him the fine parchment and told him the power of its words.

"Read it to me!" demanded the king.

One of the leaders read three or four columns of the scroll. The king was enraged. "No. This cannot be true."

With the slash of a small knife, he cut away what had just been read and threw it into the fire.

"Stop!" cried the leaders in horror. "This scroll contains the words of Comfort-Giver. We ask that you not destroy it."

A wicked smile crossed the king's lips as he watched the skin on which the words were written scorch and curl and blacken into ash. "Read on."

Three or four columns later, the king cried, "No! No! No!"

Again he cut away what had been read and threw it into his fire. When the leaders finished reading, the entire scroll was a mass of ashes, and the acrid smell of the burning sheepskin filled the room.

"Who wrote this scroll?" demanded the king.

"Weeping Prophet dictated it to his assistant," said one of the leaders.

"Bring them both to me!"

Soldiers searched the city and surrounding hills, but the two men could not be found.

Hidden in a secret cave not far from the city, the prophet felt a breeze float by. "Take another scroll and have all of my words rewritten. Then when the king's wrath has cooled, go to him with these words: 'You burned my scroll and threatened my prophet, so you will die. Your body will be thrown to the ground where it will lie in the heat of day and the frost of night.' "

"I shall do whatever you ask," said Weeping Prophet.

Now the Kingdom of the Dragon stretched itself westward. Its shadow fell upon the New Land. For three summers, Tribute King paid his silver and gold to Dragon King rather than Delta King. But then Delta King rebuilt his army and pushed the dragon back. With these two kingdoms locked in battle, the time seemed right to rebel. So Tribute King turned his back on the dragon and sent no silver and gold to the east.

But Dragon King had a watchful eye and refused to allow any land, no matter how small, to thwart him. He sent raiders against the Southern Kingdom. Tribute King gathered his warriors and went out to quell these desert raiders, but a spear through the heart fulfilled the prophet's words. His body was thrown to the ground by his mighty stallion as the raiders forced the kingdom's warriors back across the Winding River. There the king's body lay in the heat of day and the frost of night.

The Army of Dragon King soon joined the raiders. These forces surrounded the City of Palms. Inside the walls, the son of Tribute King was crowned. He was a young man, but he also hated Weeping Prophet. He was known as Winter King because of the time of year and the coldness of his heart.

For three cycles of the moon, the Army of the Dragon pounded the walls. A sea of enemy soldiers swept around the city. The keepers of the Special Place remembered the prophet's words, while the leaders of the kingdom remembered his scroll. All had been foretold.

"A choice lies before you," called Dragon King to Winter King. "You can watch your city fall and your people die, or you can surrender. If you lay down your swords and open wide your gates, I will treat all your people, including the royal family, with respect."

The city was silent.

The gates slowly opened.

The siege was over.

Winter King and his mother and all his officials walked into the hands of their enemies. The treasures of the Special Place and the royal palace were taken away to the City of Stars, the capital of the Dragon Kingdom. Ten thousand men were led away toward the east—officers and soldiers, nobles and craftsmen, keepers and merchants, and leaders of the people. At the front of this great serpentine line that faced east from the City of Palms walked Winter King and his wives. He too went to the City of Stars, where he lived the rest of his days.

Only the poorest people were left.

Among them was the Weeping Prophet.

IF ONE BREAKS HIS WORD
TWICE,
THERE IS NO NEED
FOR A THIRD TEST.

CHAPTER 8

THE FINAL KING

Book King had three sons. Tribute King died in battle with the King-dom of the Dragon. Cedar King died in prison in the Land of Deltas. His third son remained in the City of Palms.

"Your kingdom still believes in the Dynasty of the Shepherd," said Dragon King. "I will make you king of your people if you will sign a treaty of total loyalty."

"I pledge myself and all my people to be faithful servants of the great and powerful Dragon King," said the third son.

Early the next morning, on the steps of the royal palace, Dragon King crowned the third son as the Final King of the Southern Kingdom.

The next year the new king sent an envoy of allegiance to the City of Stars. Weeping Prophet sent along a letter to the exiles that had been taken across the Great River:

"Comfort-Giver says to build houses and settle down; plant gardens and eat what they produce.

"Marry those who look beyond the sky.

"Have healthy sons and daughters.

"Teach them what is right.

"You shall live in this distant kingdom for seventy summers. But the one who holds stars in his hands wishes you to have prosperity, not to come to harm. Call out his name, and he will come to you and return you to your land."

This letter was read to the exiles and they were greatly encouraged.

Several summers later, Final King was tempted by his advisors to break his vow of allegiance.

"Dragon King has taken our people and our treasures," said a chief advisor. "They are our enemies and we must resist them."

"But we have a treaty of loyalty," said the king.

"Treaties are broken all the time. Nobody expects you to keep it."

"But how can we stand if we defy the dragon?"

"The Land of Deltas hates the dragon as much as we do," said the chief advisor. "Send an envoy south to get horses and weapons and warriors. Then we can free our people and recapture our treasures."

"Do not listen to your advisors," interrupted Weeping Prophet; "listen to the one who is infinite and eternal and all-powerful. Be true to your treaty and serve Dragon King. If you rebel or resist or refuse to do right, the one above all will send sword and famine and plague. Let our treaty stand and our people remain until Comfort-Giver comes for them. Then he will bring the captives back and restore them to their land."

"Do not listen to Weeping Prophet," said the advisors. "We are a proud people and should not allow any kingdom to turn us into servants."

In the end, Final King listened to his advisors and rejected the words of the prophet. He broke his treaty and sent an envoy to the Land of Deltas. Delta King was angry at the dragon and was generous and eager to assist any who would stand against the mighty kingdom. He sent horses and weapons and warriors to Final King.

Spies watched all that was happening in the City of Palms and sent their reports back to their homeland. Dragon King responded swiftly to crush the rebellion before it got started. Then he demanded that Final King come to the City of Stars or be dethroned.

"What shall I do?" the king asked.

His advisors debated but came to no conclusion.

"You must go," insisted Weeping Prophet. "You made a treaty of total loyalty and you have been untrue. Now is the time to go to Dragon King and bow before him.

"Humble your heart.

"Admit your wrong.

"Beg forgiveness."

"But look what Dragon King has done to our people."

"No," said the prophet, "it is what our people have done to themselves. This is the result of our foolishness, but ultimately the Kingdom of the Dragon will not go unpunished."

"If I go, will I return?" asked the king.

"You will return if you do as I say."

"I shall go and bow before him and do as you have said."

"There is one more thing," said the prophet. "My assistant has a brother who is an officer in your army. Take him with you, and let him carry this scroll to read to the exiles."

"What is written on this scroll?"

The prophet unrolled the scroll and began to read. "When the time is right, Comfort-Giver will repay the Kingdom of the Dragon for all the wrongs done to our people. A land to their east will ambush them and lay waste to the great dragon. The thick walls of the City of Stars will be leveled and its high gates set on fire. Cries will fill the air, and then all will fall silent. Then the city will be a heap of ruins, a haunt of jackals."

"I will have your assistant's brother read the scroll," assured the king.

"After it is read, he must tie it to a heavy stone and throw it into the Great River. In such a way the Kingdom of the Dragon will sink and rise no more."

Final King did all Weeping Prophet said. Within a cycle of the moon, the king had been forgiven and the scroll read and the exiles were encouraged.

Several summers later, the king's advisors pressured him to again break his treaty of allegiance with the dragon and stand with Delta King.

"Dragon King is too busy to notice," said the advisors. "We must do something to free our people."

"You have a treaty," said the prophet, "and Comfort-Giver has asked you not to break it. Be patient. He will free your people when he said he would."

Final King looked to the advisors.

Then to the prophet.

Then back to the advisors.

Runners were immediately sent to the Land of Deltas to report that the Southern Kingdom was now its ally.

"Because you have not listened to Comfort-Giver," said Weeping Prophet, "this city is about to be taken by Dragon King. Its walls will be breached and its buildings burned. You will be captured," his finger pointed steadfastly at the king, "and carried away to face the one to which you twice pledged total alliance."

"Remove him!" ordered the king.

Four fierce royal guards grabbed the prophet and threw him from the palace and slammed the thick, wooden doors on him. People stared as Weeping Prophet stood and dusted off his clothing. As he walked the city streets, he repeated all that he had said to the king.

By winter the massive Army of the Dragon crossed the fertile crescent and marched toward the City of Palms. The Blue Planet trembled as soldiers and horses and equipment made their way toward the setting sun. The army encamped outside the city and cut it off. Within days, powerful battering rams pounded the walls and gates.

Final King stood in the watchtowers and realized he was doomed. Why had he followed the false words of his advisors? Why hadn't he listened to Weeping Prophet?

The king sent runners to the prophet, saying, "Speak to Comfort-Giver on our behalf. Beg him to save us from our enemies like he has done in times past."

"I warned you," said the prophet, "and you chose another way. It is too late to stop the destruction. Those who stay in this city will face sword and famine and plague, but those who surrender will live."

But before Final King could respond, runners from the south announced that Delta King was leading a large army from the Land of Pyramids. In a few days this force would arrive, and the city would be safe.

The king smiled.

The people celebrated.

The advisors gloated.

Weeping Prophet went to the king and spoke the words of Comfort-Giver. "Do not be deceived. The Delta Army which has come to support you will soon return to its own land. Then the Dragon Army will return. It will attack this city and capture it and burn it."

The people were angry at the prophet and refused to let him ruin their celebration. After the Delta Army arrived and the Dragon Army had withdrawn, Weeping Prophet started to leave the city. But when he reached the city gate, the captain of the guard arrested him.

"You are a traitor," said the captain, "and now you are deserting your people to join the dragon."

"That is not true. I am leaving the city to do some business a few hours to the north."

The captain would not listen to him. He took the prophet to his commander, who had him beaten and thrown into an underground prison. Through several cycles of the moon the prophet was treated badly. Meanwhile the Delta Army returned to its own land, and the Dragon Army resumed its strangling siege.

Final King saw how the words of the prophet were fulfilled, so he had him secretly brought to the palace.

"Are there any more words from Comfort-Giver?" asked the king.

"Shall I speak the truth?"

"Yes."

"In two summers you will be captured and handed over to Dragon King. These are the words of Comfort-Giver."

"You have great courage to speak to your king in such a way. I could end your life with one word. But instead I will place you in the palace stockade, where you can see the sun and eat fresh bread."

Several cycles of the moon passed, and the leaders of the kingdom came to the king. "Weeping Prophet should be put to death. He is trying to convince the guards in the royal stockade to surrender. He says, 'It is too late to stop the destruction. Those who stay in this city will face sword and famine and plague, but those who surrender will live!' "

"He is in your hands," said the king. "I can do nothing to oppose you."

So the leaders took the prophet and lowered him by ropes deep into a cistern of the royal stockade. He sank to his knees in the thick mud.

Days later a royal official went to the king. "Weeping Prophet has done nothing wrong. Yet the wicked leaders have thrown him into a cistern where he will starve to death."

"Remove him before he dies," said the king.

So the official and the men lifted the prophet out of the cistern. Then the king secretly sent for the prophet. Once again he asked, "Are there any more words from Comfort-Giver?"

"If I speak the truth, will you have me thrown back into the cistern, or will you allow the leaders of the city to take my life?"

"I give you my guarantee you shall be safe."

"As you gave your guarantee to Dragon King?"

The king hung his head in shame.

"Comfort-Giver says that if you surrender to Dragon King

"you will be spared;

"your children will live;

"your city will not be burned."

But Final King hardened his heart and refused to surrender. He spat on the ground and wished he had not promised Weeping Prophet safety.

The prophet was taken back to the royal stockade, and there he stayed until the day the City of Palms was broken.

CHAPTER 9

THE BROKEN CITY

The fruits and vegetables were now completely gone. So were the animals that could be eaten for meat and the flour that could be made into bread. There was little water, let alone wine. Children stood on the street corners and begged for crusts. People traded bags of silver and gold for a mouthful of food. Old men fell lifeless. Horses and donkeys and camels were slaughtered, but soon they were all gone. People grew desperate enough that they broke into the houses of their neighbors, looking for scraps of food. Women searched for rats and snakes and insects, anything to fill their families' aching emptiness. People died daily. Rumors spread that some of the dead had even been eaten.

After two years of sword and famine and plague, the City of Palms still refused to surrender. The Army of the Dragon found a weak spot in the northern wall. That summer they moved the battering rams into place and smashed into the thick stone with thunderous blows that shook the heart of the city. Day and night they pounded. Week after week they pounded.

The mortar crumbled.

The stones shifted.

The wall fell.

"These are my orders," said Dragon King to his chief commander. "Capture the people of substance and take them to our land. Find Final King and bind him in bronze shackles and bring him to me. Also bring all the keepers and leaders and royal advisors. But when you find Weeping Prophet, do not harm him. Instead, do for him whatever he asks."

There was little left in the city when the commander led his warriors through the breach. The soldiers of the south fought fiercely, but the situation was hopeless. Most fell to the sword before the call to retreat was sounded. When the soldiers fled, the streets were left defenseless. The people of the city were too weary and hungry to resist, so they were easily captured. Soon they would join those who had been captured some ten summers before. But the keepers and leaders and royal advisors were not treated so kindly. They were arrested with more roughness than was necessary and told that the next day they would learn their fate.

By nightfall, Final King and the remnant of his army still had not been found. As the sun tucked itself beneath the horizon, they escaped through a southern gate near the palace gardens and made their way toward the Winding River. Somehow in a night darker than most, the king got separated from his men and was captured the next day near the Fortress City. He was immediately placed in bronze shackles and taken to Dragon King, where his sentence was pronounced.

The keepers of the sanctuary were brought before him, and Dragon King's elite guards cut them down. Final King was not moved. The leaders of the Southern Kingdom were brought before him, and the guards cut them down. Final King shook his head in sadness. Next came the royal advisors he had tried so hard to please. They were brought before him, and the guards cut them down. Final King tightened his jaw and held his emotions.

Then the soldiers brought his sons before him.

"No, not them!" he cried. "I will do anything if you will only spare my sons."

"Two times you pledged your loyalty to Dragon King," said the executioner, "and two times you broke your word. You have been weak and indecisive. You have been untrue. Therefore the last thing your eyes will see is this."

Dragon King gave the signal, and his guards ended the lives of Final King's sons. Final King's heart shattered. He fell to his knees and embraced the still-warm bodies as a deep cry pierced the air.

Then two guards gagged the king and grabbed his arms and lifted him to his feet. Another guard lifted a razor-sharp dagger, and Final King prepared for death. But instead, the tallest guard leaned forward and blinded him in both eyes. Within days he was taken across the fertile crescent and imprisoned in the City of Stars, where he lived in darkness until his death.

A cycle of the moon after the wall fell, the commander entered the Special Place and took from it everything of value, even the ark of mystery with its golden angels. Articles of silver and gold and bronze were placed in large wooden wagons to be carried back to the Kingdom of the Dragon. The soldiers stripped the royal palace of all it held and looted the city. When nothing within the walls had any worth, soldiers set fire to the sanctuary and the royal palace and every building that held its ground.

Flames climbed high.

Smoke turned the sky black.

Heat pushed the soldiers back.

While the Army of the Dragon cheered and laughed, the captives wept. Their beautiful city was burning. Their mighty capital had stood for some four hundred summers, but now it lay in ruins. Their kingdom was no more.

Several days later, the commander and his entire army went to the large breach in the city's north wall. There they tore down every stone until the City of Palms was left unprotected.

With nothing more to do, the commander directed the captives toward the Mountains of the Dawn. As the people began their journey, the commander saw Weeping Prophet chained among the captives and remembered the words of Dragon King.

"Today you shall be free," said the commander. "You may come with me to the City of Stars or you may stay in this land. You may go wherever you please."

"I shall stay," said the prophet, "for this is the land of Comfort-Giver."

So the commander gave him food and clothing and silver. Weeping Prophet thanked him and said good-bye to all the captives. Then he walked toward his fallen city and those who had been left behind. For Dragon King had ordered the poorest of the poor to remain in the land so they might

plow the fields,

prune the orchards,

and tend the vineyards.

The prophet looked west to the broken walls of what had once been the most beautiful city on the Blue Planet. He passed through the shattered stones and splintered gates with a head bent in pain. The streets, once busy and full of people, were now quiet and deserted. At night the wild animals would soon prowl the emptiness.

The prophet stepped between heaps of ash and rubble. Smoke hung about the ruins as vultures and ravens circled above. He wiped away the tears, but they returned before his face was dry. Young and old lay dead in the dust of cluttered streets. He wished to bury them and protect them from scavengers, but there were too many bodies. The stench burned his nose and turned his stomach. He looked away and made his way toward the Special Place. He knew what he had predicted, and now he saw that it had all come true. The sanctuary was no more. Even its remains had been leveled.

Weeping Prophet fell facedown into the ashes where the ark of mystery had once rested. A cry of unbridled grief echoed through the desolation as a river flowed from his heart. He tore his clothes and threw a fistful of dirt toward the sky. He pounded the ground with anger and pain and bitterness.

"He has abandoned us.

"His glory has left.

"His splendor has departed."

Jackals looked up at the one who invaded their domain, and a snake smiled at all that surrounded him. This, thought Shining One, was one of his finest hours, for the city on which Comfort-Giver had put so much attention was destroyed.

Weeping Prophet lifted his head as his eyes overflowed until he could not even see the smoldering destruction before him.

"We are orphans. Our joy has passed away and our dancing has turned to tears."

As the sun set and the world turned dark, the prophet stood alone among the glowing embers of his broken city. His heart ached and there was no one to dry his bitter tears.

He looked beyond the sky and cried, "Where is Comfort-Giver?"

Jackals broke the silence with their hungry howls. There was a strange silence to the still sky, but the truth teller knew that it was not that Comfort-Giver did not care about what had happened. No, even the one above all must be grieving.

"I know if I wait patiently, there will be hope."

The prophet stood still as his heart pounded and his eyes stung.

Moments passed and then he felt it. The faintest whisper of a gentle breeze washed his face. And the words of Comfort-Giver were carried on the breeze.

"I gave you a new promise, the same promise given at the fall of the Northern Kingdom."

"What is your promise?"

"Look to the stars with the greatest fire."

The prophet searched the night sky and said, "I see them. Yes, I see them."

"These are to remind you," whispered the wind, "that no matter how dark the path, I will always show you the way."

The prophet smiled as joy sparkled again in his wet and weary eyes.

"Restore us to your heart.

"Return us to your infinite love.

"Renew our days as of old."

Now the cool night breeze became a wind that wrapped around the Weeping Prophet and held him in the strongest of arms and gave him peace that went beyond words. "All this shall happen and much more.

"Much, much more."

EPILOGUE

A chill had fallen over the night. Some ewes had given birth during the last nine days that the old man had been speaking of the Southern Kingdom's fall. Of course all the lambs had been born in the dead of night to interrupt a shepherd's sleep. At least two more lambs would be born before this night ended, and one of the births looked as though it would be fraught with pain and difficulty.

The people hung their heads, reliving in their minds the hard night of their fallen city. The ancient storyteller felt the weariness of his years tonight, for the story of Weeping Prophet was one of the hardest to tell. Everyone was silent, even the owls and foxes.

Coals and ashes of the fire fell in upon themselves with a whoosh that sent sparks flying. Everyone glanced up and stared into the falling embers.

"He still is our Comfort-Giver," reminded the old man with a hundred wrinkles. "For it is when all is lost that one finds most the need for comfort. That's when he is close."

"But, Grandfather. . ." said the girl who had known nine summers. She tugged at his robe to get his attention.

"What is it, little one?"

"How can there be any comfort for us?" she asked.

"We have no king

"and no kingdom

"and we lost our City of Palms."

"Aaah," he said soothingly, looking down into her dark eyes. "But the stories are not yet finished."

"I know," said the girl-child with a smile. "There is much more."

"And there is hope," the storyteller added.

PART 3
THE HEART-LIFTER

TABLE OF CONTENTS
THE HEART-LIFTER

Prologue 121

1. The Fire Walkers (Daniel 1–3) 123

2. The Watchman (Ezekiel) 129

3. The Mysterious Hand (Daniel 4–5) 135

4. The Dark Den (Daniel 6, 9) 141

5. The Rebuilding (Ezra 1–6) 147

6. The Maiden Queen (Esther 1–4) 153

7. The Saving (Esther 5–10) 159

8. The Teacher (Ezra 7–10; Nehemiah 1) 165

9. The Wall Builder (Nehemiah 2–4, 6–12) 172

10. The Conqueror and the Madman (1 Maccabees 1–2) 178

11. The Hammer (1 Maccabees 3–6:17) 184

12. The Brothers (1 Maccabees 6–16) 190

13. The Future (Isaiah 7–11, 52–53; Micah, Zechariah) 197

Epilogue 203

PROLOGUE

The sun set behind the ancient city that lay some miles distant in the highlands. The shepherds loved it when their tents were pitched so close to their capital, the most beloved of all cities. Here the grass was more plentiful.

Several older women carefully arranged the night's scant portion of fig and olive branches in the fire pit. The oldest of the women lit the tinder and gently blew the twigs alight. Soon women and children gathered around in a tight circle, absorbing the heat and light on a night that promised to be unseasonably crisp. A few men and boys shared the fire this night, but their lives were harder in lambing season, and most would soon spend all of their nights with the flocks. Even tonight, those who had come to be with their families would walk back in the dark with a late supper for the shepherd watchmen.

The storyteller with the long, gray beard stepped forward and took his seat on a flat rock. None knew his age, but he had known far more summers than most men ever see. And it seemed his step was still light, lighter now than when he told the stories of the fall of the City of Palms. He was "Grandfather," the elder in their tent community, though he was not of any of their clans. He had lived most of his years in another community not many miles away, among the harsh wilderness and canyons and cliffs west of the Salty Sea.

He smiled warmly at his friends.

"This is where the stories change," began the old man. "Our people were very low, but he who is beyond the sky was always there among them in their darkest captivity. Soon their time came for release and returning and rebuilding."

"I think these are the most important stories of all," said one shepherd, who anticipated the joy of what was about to be told.

"No story is more important than the others," the storyteller corrected. "All were given by the one who is infinite and eternal and all-powerful. All are about when our fathers have walked in his presence."

The old man paused and rubbed the hundred wrinkles of his face thoughtfully.

"I am mistaken," he said. "One story is most the important of any since Man and Woman stood with Garden-Maker, but it cannot be fully told.

"But never mind, for that will be the last story. Meanwhile other stories will lift our hearts, though they also tell of hard days and defeats and death."

"We are ready," said the shepherd.

"So is the one who holds stars in his hands." The storyteller smiled broadly and stood to speak.

> HOWEVER INTENSE THE FLAME,
> THE INDESTRUCTIBLE
> CAN NEVER BE BURNED.

CHAPTER 1

THE FIRE WALKERS

During the days of Book King, a child was born to a noble family in the City of Palms. As summers passed, the boy grew strong and handsome. He was sharp of mind and large of heart and loved by all who knew him. His eyes focused on the eternal beyond the Blue Planet, so he was known as Sky. But in time that was looked upon with less and less favor.

Book King was killed.

Cedar King was taken prisoner.

Tribute King ruled.

Early in the reign of this king, the Army of the Dragon chased the Army of the Pyramids back to the deltas. As Dragon King passed the City of Palms, the bravest warriors of Comfort-Giver marched out to meet them. Sky and his three closest friends held their silver swords high. The Dragon Army drew the faithful fighters away from the city and surrounded them. The soldiers were captured and stripped of their armor and placed in bronze shackles.

They were sent across the fertile crescent to the magnificent City of Stars. The capital of the Kingdom of the Dragon straddled the Great River and was linked by a six-tiered bridge. The most amazing building within the double walls was the temple to the dragon with its golden walls and alabaster pillars and cedar roof beams.

Captives were treated respectfully but guarded carefully. Sky and his three friends did all they could to stay together. Every morning, they spoke to the one who holds stars in his hands. They asked for strength and courage and wisdom.

"I will give you all that you ask," said the wind that swept in from the windows high above them.

"But many of the captives are downhearted," said Sky. "How can I encourage them?"

"Tell them to look at me. I am their Comfort-Giver, and I will be their Heart-Lifter."

Sky's words greatly encouraged the captives.

Dragon King called the chief palace official to his throne room, which sparkled with a thousand glazed bricks of blue and white and yellow.

"Choose for me the best of the captives," ordered the king; "young leaders who are strong and handsome, intelligent and teachable, respected and understanding."

The chief palace official carefully studied the young men from the Southern Kingdom and chose those who met the king's requirements. Among those selected were Sky and his three friends.

"Very good," said the king as he appraised the group of young men before him. "Take these and teach them all we know. After three years of rigorous training, I will place them in positions of responsibility throughout my kingdom."

These men were given comfortable quarters with special privileges. They received silver platters overflowing with the richest food and golden goblets of the finest wine. The men stuffed themselves greedily with the delicacies set before them—all except Sky and his friends.

"Why aren't you eating?" asked the chief palace official.

"The food and wine smell wonderful," said Sky, "but the one above all has told us to eat only vegetables and to drink only water."

"But if you do not eat what is provided, the king will be offended," said the chief official.

"Why does Dragon King wish us to eat rich food and fine wine?" asked Sky.

"So you will stay strong and healthy."

"May I suggest a test?" Sky asked with utmost respect.

"Speak your mind," said the chief official.

"Give us nothing but vegetables to eat and water to drink. Then compare our strength and health with those who eat from the king's table."

After ten days, the four young men were stronger and healthier than any of the others. Thereafter they ate and drank whatever they chose.

During the next three years, the best teachers of the Kingdom of the Dragon taught them language and literature, law and history, numbers and science and stars. But the one beyond all gave his knowledge and understanding to the four young men. To Sky, Heart-Lifter added a special ability to interpret the most difficult of dreams and visions.

One night Dragon King had restless dreams. He awoke sweating and troubled and unable to sleep. His heart was full of fear. Before the sun rose above the Mountains of the Dawn, he called the wisest men before him to ease his heart.

"I have had a frightful dream." he said as he sat uneasily upon his throne, "and I need to know immediately what it means."

"Tell us your dream, and we will interpret it," said the wise men.

"I recall nothing, except that it made my heart quake."

"But if we do not know your dream, how can we interpret it?"

"You are the wisest in the land, and you say you possess secret knowledge. Are you all liars? Tell me my dream and what it means, or I will cut each one of you into pieces and turn your houses into heaps of rubble."

"No one can do such a thing," cried the wise men.

The king's face was red.

He stood from his throne.

He screamed at the wise men.

"Then you will die with every man in this city I have honored as wise. Execute them before the sun trades places with the moon."

Guards stepped forward and arrested the wise men in the room. Guards searched the city for those the king had set apart for their wisdom.

"Why have I been arrested? I was not given a chance to tell the king his dream and interpret it," said Sky.

"The wise men said it is impossible," said the commander of the guards.

"Nothing is impossible with Heart-Lifter," said Sky. "He knows the king's dream and what it means."

The commander told the king what the young man had said. Then Sky was brought bound before him.

"Is this true?" asked Dragon King.

"Heart-Lifter will tell you about your dream. Allow me to join my three friends, and I will ask Heart-Lifter to show me all you ask."

"Release him!" ordered the king.

So Sky and his three friends spoke to Heart-Lifter. Late that night, the one above all showed the king's dream. Sky went to the commander of the guards.

"I will now tell the king what he wants to know."

Sky again stood before the king. He described Dragon King's dream as if it were his own. He revealed the meaning behind the images.

The king was amazed.

He bowed down in honor.

He gave gifts to Sky.

"It was not I who saw your dream and discovered its meaning," protested Sky. "Heart-Lifter is the one who deserves your honor."

"Heart-Lifter must be great if he is able to reveal such mysteries," said the king.

"He is infinite and eternal and all-powerful."

"Because of what you have done, I make you a ruler of my kingdom and the leader of every wise man within my realm."

"I have three friends who are wise beyond their years. I ask that they might also be given positions to assist me in all that I do."

"Your request is granted," declared the king.

Sky and his friends ruled well. Their wisdom and understanding and knowledge brought them great respect. But it also stirred jealousy.

"How can we allow outsiders to rule over us?"

"This is neither right nor fair."

"There must be a way to bring about their fall."

Shining One listened to these words with delight. He took every opportunity to fan the frustration and jealousy. Then one day he had an idea.

"You are the greatest king of all the Blue Planet," said the snake as it coiled itself around the leg of the throne. "You are only missing one thing."

"What is that?" asked the king.

"You need a monument like those in the Land of Pyramids. If you only had a grand image that would remind all within your realm of how great and mighty and powerful you are."

Dragon King ordered the best craftsmen in all his land to build a giant image of himself on the main road south of the City of Stars. After years of planning and labor, there arose a statue of the king as high as the tallest cedar and as wide as six full-grown men. Once the statue was finished, a layer of the finest gold was hammered over the entire surface. It glowed in the midday sun with such intensity that it could be seen for many miles.

On the day of its dedication, every advisor and every judge and every official of the kingdom was called to stand before the king's golden image. In the cool of the evening, as the sun hung on the western horizon, the king's messenger unrolled an elegant scroll and read to the crowd.

"From this moment, whenever the royal musicians play my song, all who hear it must fall facedown and worship this beautiful statue. Whoever refuses to fall will be thrown into a blazing furnace."

As the scroll was rolled, the royal musicians played the king's song. All who stood before the golden statue fell to the ground.

During the next cycle of the moon, rumors passed through the City of Stars that Sky and his three friends would not fall facedown when the music played. Jealous leaders smiled and ran to Dragon King.

"These men from the Southern Kingdom do not obey your decrees and have no respect for your crown. If you do not squelch them, their rebellion will spread."

Furious, Dragon King ordered these men be brought to the palace. Sky was far away on royal business, but his three friends stood before the king.

"Is what I hear true?" he demanded. "Do you refuse to bow facedown before my statue when the royal musicians play?"

"It is true," said the three.

"Do you not understand that those who refuse to fall are to be thrown into a blazing furnace?"

"We understand," said the three. "But if we are thrown into a furnace, Heart-Lifter will either rescue us or he will take us to his home beyond the sky."

Anger and hatred and violence distorted Dragon King's face. "Arrest them!" he ordered. "Have the royal smelting furnace heated hotter than ever before."

Guards tied the hands and feet of the three men. Servants brought armloads of well-seasoned wood and threw them into the furnace until the flames were hot enough to melt the hardest ore.

Dragon King accompanied the condemned to the furnace. The heat pushed them back, turning skin red and singeing the hair off their faces.

"Throw them in!" demanded the king.

Guards grabbed the arms of the three and threw them into the flames, but waves of heat burst from the door so intense that the guards themselves were struck down. Their armor melted and their flesh burned and their screams distracted the king from the three who fell into the center of the blazing furnace. But when he looked up, he saw the three young men. They were alive and standing in the midst of the flames.

Everybody looked where the king pointed.

"How many men were thrown into the furnace?" shouted the king.

"Three!" answered the commander of the guards.

"Look!" The king was pale, and his pointing finger shook. "Four walk about in the furnace, and the fourth has the appearance of an angel."

Dragon King walked fearfully toward the entrance. In a trembling voice he cried, "Come out. Please, come out."

The three young men stepped from the fire, and the fourth disappeared. Amazed advisors and judges and officials surrounded the friends of Sky.

Their hair was not singed.

Their clothes were not scorched.

They did not even smell of smoke.

The only effect of the flames was that their binding ropes had burned away.

"How did you walk through the flames without being harmed?" asked the king.

"Heart-Lifter sent an angel to protect us from the flames."

Dragon King fell facedown and cried out, "Heart-Lifter is above all."

When Sky returned and heard what had happened, he wept.

"Why are you sad?" asked his three friends.

"If I had not been called away," wept Sky, "I could have walked the fire with you."

ONE CAN LOOK AWAY FROM TRUTH
OR STOP ONE'S EARS,
BUT THAT IN NO WAY
DIMINISHES ITS REALITY.

CHAPTER 2

THE WATCHMAN

My wife is sick and childless. Let us stay," begged the solidly built man with piercing brown eyes and long, black hair. "I am but a lowly keeper of the sanctuary."

"You must follow Winter King to the Kingdom of the Dragon," ordered the commander of the guards.

"But I am nobody."

"We have learned that the people of the Southern Kingdom have great abilities, especially those who follow the one who holds stars in his hands."

"Where did you learn this?"

"Four young men have taught us much about the one who is above all."

The man placed his arm around his wife. Together they walked many days toward the Mountains of the Dawn. They crossed the Great River and stood before Dragon King with ten thousand fellow captives.

"This land is your new home and I am your king," he said, adding, "but Sky and his friends have told me about Heart-Lifter.

"So look beyond the sky

"and listen to his voice

"and walk where he leads."

The captives felt drops of rain wash their dusty faces as their cheers echoed off the city walls. Then the sun broke through.

"Look!" shouted the man with long, black hair. The most beautiful rainbow these people had ever seen graced the heavens.

"Who remembers what it means?" asked a man of nobility who stood beside Dragon King. It was Sky himself. He went on to urge his country-men, "Look to the heavens, for this is a reminder of Heart-Lifter's first promise: He is always close and he will always care."

The people were sent throughout the Kingdom of the Dragon. The strong, young man with long, black hair went south of the City of Stars to work the land. He plowed and planted and irrigated a small field next to the long canal linking the Great River and the Golden River.

One day he sat alone on the quiet banks of the canal, dangling his feet in the muddy water. As a slight breeze rippled the waters, he recalled ancient stories from the Book of Beginnings. Man had first looked into the gentle eyes of Woman in a luscious garden that now lay buried beneath the sand some two or three days from where he sat. Builder had made his giant boat not far from this exact spot. Merchant was born and married and first heard the voice of the wind in the City of the Moon, a day to the south. A strange rumble interrupted this reverie.

The rumble began low and deep.

It grew louder and louder.

It shook and rattled all about him.

In the distance, a mighty windstorm rolled across the plain from the north. This churning, billowing thundercloud moved closer with a mo-mentum that seemed neither natural nor normal. At first the cloud seemed black and threatening with the brightness of the desert sun biting at its edges. Jagged lightning struck out in all directions. But the center of the cloud began to burn like the noonday sun. A swirling storm of light now stopped before the man. His eyes were transfixed by the dazzling splendor of four angels who moved on powerful wings at the center of this storm. The angels stood back to back to back to back with their wings touching and their chests directed outward.

He was amazed to see that each angel had four faces. The one looking out was a man; the one to the right was a lion; the one to the left was an ox; the one looking back was an eagle. These angels glowed like flaming torches and bolts of fire flashed from each. The sound of their wings was like. . .

the roar of rushing waters,

the bellow of rolling thunder,

the force of an invincible army.

As he looked, trembling, down from their faces, he saw a wheel within a wheel beneath the four angels. The rims were inlaid with translucent gemstones that twinkled like a thousand eyes. The wheels moved in every direction, sparkling as they spun. When the wheels went forward, so did the angels.

Above the angels was a bejeweled throne that surely was more beautiful than any upon the Blue Planet. On this throne sat a figure who shone with a light so brilliant and pure and awesome that the man fell facedown and covered his eyes with his hands.

"Stand, and I will speak to you," came a resounding voice.

Fearfully the man with the long, black hair rose to his feet, but he kept his head bent and his eyes focused on the ground.

"You are Watchman. I send you to watch over my people. Speak my words, though they will stir up anger as fierce as scorpions and division as sharp as thorns. Be not afraid, for I shall protect you as you warn my people of dangers that approach their hearts."

The voice fell silent, and the ground stopped its shaking. Watchman looked up to see that the cloud was gone and the lightning had ceased and the day was still. Had it been a dream? No, what he had glimpsed was reality itself. All else was dreamlike in comparison. So he set out toward the villages of his people. He had both the message and also a way to gain a hearing from the downcast people. Watchman acted out the message as well as told it.

On a huge clay tablet he drew a map of the City of Palms and laid it in front of his house. Interested people drifted by, watching as he spent hours building a wall of sand and soil around his miniature city, making it as accurate as he could recall. Tears dampened faces as onlookers recognized their beloved city.

The next day more came to see Watchman set up tiny tents around the walls. He built siege works and portable ramps and battering rams with which to assault the city.

"What are you doing?" asked the crowd.

"See the future of the City of Palms," said Watchman.

"What will happen to our brothers and sisters?"

"Some will die by plague and famine.

"Some will be struck down by swordsmen.

"Some will join us as captives of Dragon King."

"You are wrong," shouted someone in the crowd. "The City of Palms will never fall."

Watchman reached out and smashed down his hand, opening a breach in the tiny north wall. "It will fall. The king will be captured and the sanctuary ransacked and the glory will depart."

The people would not accept such words. They refused to believe Watchman.

A wind blew about the man with the long, black hair and whispered in his ear, "They have not listened to my words, and they will not listen to your words. Speak no more until you hear that the City of Palms has fallen."

The man became silent.

His tongue did not move.

He uttered no words.

Heart-Lifter sometimes came with words for his people. Then the man with the long, black hair spoke of the one who holds stars in his hands. On all other days, he worked in silence. Early one morning, as the sun touched the Mountains of the Dawn, Watchman walked with his maker and listened.

"Today the siege has started," whispered the voice of the wind. "Dragon King has surrounded the City of Palms. Write down this date on a clay tablet. Tell my people that this is the beginning of the end of their kingdom."

Watchman spoke, but still none listened.

"The time has come to act," said the wind to his watchman. "I shall not hold back. I shall not have pity. I shall not relent. The king will be captured and the sanctuary ransacked and the glory will depart."

Watchman spoke, but when the people refused to believe, his silence returned. Then three years later, in the middle of the night, Watchman yawned and Heart-Lifter touched his lips.

He was no longer silent.

His tongue moved freely.

He shouted for joy.

The next day a man, ragged and dusty and exhausted, pounded on the door, crying, "The City of Palms has fallen!"

"How do you know such a thing?" asked Watchman.

"I was a palace guard to Final King. I saw it with my own eyes. The king was captured and the sanctuary ransacked and the glory has departed."

"When did it fall?"

"Six cycles of the moon ago, Dragon King breached the northern wall."

"When did Dragon King surround the city and lay siege to it?" The palace guard told Watchman the day and month and year. Watchman turned and walked into his house. He returned clutching a baked clay tablet. On the tablet was written the same day and month and year that the palace guard had said.

The captives of the Kingdom of the Dragon wept when they heard. Without the City of Palms, their kingdom was no more. All that Watchman had said was true. The people hung their heads and felt rejected and desolate and hopeless. The one beyond the sky saw how their hearts were broken. He came to Watchman with heart-lifting words.

"Heart-Lifter longs to bring you back to a time of blessings. His people are wandering sheep who have been scattered over the Blue Planet, while wild beasts seek their destruction. But Heart-Lifter will search for the lost and rescue the strays. He will carry the injured and strengthen the weak and heal the sick. He will bring them back to their land. He will guide them to high pastures where the grass is green and the water sweet. There they can live in safety and peace and prosperity. He still is our Shepherd."

"But our hearts are shriveled and our bones are dry," said the people. "Our spirits are too dead to follow the maker of all."

"Heart-Lifter is the giver of life," said Watchman, "and he promises you a new life—richer and fuller and more abundant."

"How is this possible?" asked the people as they shook their heads and shuffled off.

"Impossibilities have never kept Heart-Lifter from keeping his word," Watchman called out to those who walked away.

The air grew quiet and the wind wrapped itself around the man with the long, black hair. As it swirled, he closed his eyes. His spirit was transported to a desert valley—barren and hostile and empty. There was no shade in this dry and thirsty land, only piles of sun-bleached bones picked clean by vultures and jackals. Scorpions and lizards scattered as he walked among the bones. He bent to examine a long, thin bone. It was human, a leg bone. He gasped and let it fall.

The wind once again swirled around him. "Can dead bones live?" it asked.

Watchman thought about the question. "Yes, with you even these bones can walk again."

"Call out to the bones. Tell them I have not forgotten them. Tell them I will breathe upon them, and they will return to life."

So Watchman spoke Heart-Lifter's words to the bones as the wind rustled among the piles. The bones began to move, to rattle together and connect in their places. Muscle and flesh and skin appeared, stretching over the bones. Now thousands of whole bodies lay still and lifeless over the desert ground.

"One thing is missing," said the wind.

"They have no life," answered Watchman.

"Where can they find life?"

"You are the source."

The wind filled each mouth. Heart-Lifter's breath filled the bodies.

Chests rose and fell.

Eyes opened.

Hands moved.

Ten thousand people stood, walking about and singing to the one who holds stars in his hands. The wind wrapped itself around Watchman and said, "These dry bones are my people. They believe they are rejected and desolate and hopeless, but I shall breathe new life into them and lead them back to their land and shower them with blessings."

"What must we do?"

"Be patient and look beyond the sky."

As Watchman looked up, the sky turned black and a thousand stars spelled out Heart-Lifter's promise: No matter how dark the path, he will always show the way.

WHEN ONE TRIVIALIZES
WHAT IS SACRED,
ONE ULTIMATELY LOSES
WHAT IS VALUED MOST.

CHAPTER 3

THE MYSTERIOUS HAND

A tree sprouted beside a great river and grew until its top touched the sky. It grew large and strong and tall until it was the mightiest tree in all the Blue Planet. The tree was admired by all.

Its leaves were beautiful.

Its fruit was succulent.

Its shade was a blessing for all beneath its branches.

Suddenly a glowing angel with a face as bright as the sun descended from beyond the sky. "Cut down the mighty tree," he called out in a loud voice that struck terror in all who heard.

"Break off its branches.

"Strip off its leaves.

"Scatter all its fruit.

"Leave nothing of its majesty, but its stump. The grass shall surround it and the dew shall fall upon it and it shall be forgotten for seven summers."

Two powerful men with a large, sharp saw began their work. Back and forth went their saw until the mighty tree leaned precariously. It slowly tottered and began its fall.

"No!" screamed Dragon King as he sat up in his bed, sweat dripping down his face. Guards and assistants and servants came running.

"What has happened? What is wrong? What can we do?"

"I dreamed a terrible dream," said the king, his body still shaking. "It holds a message, but I do not know what it means. Go at once and bring to me the wisest men of my kingdom."

By sunrise those who could interpret dreams stood sleepily before the king. But when they heard the details of this vision, none could discern its meaning. As the morning faded into afternoon, all the wisest men had been dismissed by the disappointed king. The last man to stand before Dragon King was Sky.

"No one can discern my dream," complained the king. "Can you see the unseeable?"

"Many years ago when no one could tell you what you dreamed and what it meant, Heart-Lifter showed the meaning to me."

"Will he do it now?"

"Heart-Lifter knows all things. He will open my eyes."

So Dragon King repeated his dream, with every detail he could remember. Sky listened intently and the one above all revealed the secret meaning. Sky stood silent.

"Tell me," demanded the king. "Tell me what you see."

"You will not like what I tell you."

"Whether good or bad, interpret my dream."

"You are the mighty tree with beautiful leaves and succulent fruit," said Sky.

Dragon King smiled as he remembered the grand height and strength and majesty of the tree in his dream.

"But you are proud and think that you are greater than the one above all. So Heart-Lifter will allow a sharp saw to drop you to the ground."

Dragon King shook his head in sadness, for he knew that indeed he had become proud.

"As the stump remained, so your life will continue. But you will wander the fields alone and sleep in the dew for seven summers. When you submit to the one who holds stars in his hands, your throne will be restored."

"Can I avoid this tragedy?" asked the king.

"Humble yourself and do what is right and show compassion."

Dragon King nodded, but deep in his heart, Shining One already was making light of Sky's prediction. The fruits of his pride were simply too enjoyable to ignore.

So he ignored the frightful dream for several cycles of the moon. Then one day he stood on the roof of his palace and looked out over the City of Stars. What magnificent gardens and sparkling temples. What a vast complex of government buildings. "I have made this the most beautiful place on the Blue Planet. Even Heart-Lifter must honor my greatness."

"Fool," came a voice of doom from the sky. "You compare yourself to the one who is above all? I now withdraw my hand of blessing, and we shall see what glory is yours."

"You shall be driven from your people.

"You shall live with the wild animals.

"You shall eat the grass of the fields.

"This will continue until you recognize that without me you have nothing."

A wild, raving cry came from the king. His eyes lost their focus and his thoughts were pulled into an incoherent frenzy and his mouth babbled. Guards rushed to his aid, but the king growled and spat and swung his arms violently at them. He squatted down and leaped from the rooftop. The guards grabbed his arms in midleap and pulled him to safety, calling for help.

No servants or advisors or healers could calm him. He attacked all within reach. Locked alone in his bedchamber, he cut his arms and tore out his hair and banged his head on the walls until blood flowed from his brow.

Because Dragon King was no longer himself, his eldest son was installed as king-regent, and the father was sent from his people. This was the way in the Kingdom of the Dragon. The king wandered the fields, eating grass with the cattle and lying in the morning dew. This was his life for seven speechless years.

Then one midsummer's night he looked up. His beclouded mind saw a thousand brilliant stars and realized the greatness of the one who holds them in his hands.

At that moment the king's sanity returned, and he walked back to his city. The people ran in fear, except a few who asked cautious questions:

"Why have you returned?"

"Are you still dangerous?"

"What drove you mad?"

"My pride overcame my reason," said Dragon King. "Therefore, Heart-Lifter took both from me. I now realize that there is one far greater than I, one who is infinite and eternal and all-powerful."

The king was restored to his throne and he reigned together with his son through the rest of his days. The prosperity of the land was greater even than before.

When Dragon King grew old and gray and left the Blue Planet, his sons battled for power and lost it in the end to a relative who shared the throne with his oldest son. The new king was neither a leader nor a warrior. Soon he abandoned his kingdom and settled in an oasis on the northern edge of the Great Desert. There he bowed to the moon and studied the stars and listened to the ancient serpent.

Many years later, the Kingdom of the Bear sent an army against the Kingdom of the Dragon. They reached the walls of the City of Stars, but there they stopped. The walls were so thick and solid that they seemed impossible to breach. And the city was so large and well provisioned that a siege seemed futile.

The son of the king laughed at the enemy soldiers outside the walls. He had become a proud and stubborn lover of the ways of Shining One. He disdained what was good and right and pure. He drank much wine and mocked his maker. A thousand nobles followed his example. To show how unafraid he was, he invited the nobles to his marvelous palace. They called to Shining One and bowed to his serpentine statues. Then the king called for wine to be served in the golden goblets that Dragon King had stolen from the very sanctuary of Heart-Lifter. From these they drank until they were sick. They cursed and scorned and ridiculed.

Suddenly an arm reached in from a dark window. At first it went unnoticed as it scraped a pointed finger against the rough white plaster, leaving a blood-red mark. The marks formed a letter in a strange language, and then another. Moving slowly from right to left, the writing finger seemed to write two words, then a word below, and another word below that.

Letter by letter.

Word by word.

Line by line.

By the time the second line was half written, those near the window stared in trembling fear. By the third line, the music had stopped. A hush covered the room as every eye turned toward the mysterious hand. Suddenly the hand withdrew, but still no one moved to see who had dared invade the king's party. Finally whispers began to spread: "Who wrote it? What does it say? What does it mean?" The strange words stood as a ragged, red scrawl upon the pristine walls of royalty.

Guards rushed from the palace but could find no trace of the one who had written on the wall. Advisors studied the script and finally reported: "The language is that of the Southern Kingdom. We know what the words say, but we do not know what they mean."

The king's son called for wise men. By now he had a great pain in his head and felt sick, but not just from the wine. "Before this night is over, I must know what the words mean." He shook as he pointed at the wall. "Whoever tells me what is behind these words will be clothed in purple and be given the finest gold chain and be the highest ruler in this kingdom after me."

After much thought, the wise men all agreed that the words were meaningless. Yet each heart trembled as long as the king's son gazed upon the marks.

"Dragon King knew of one who could answer his questions when all his wise men failed," said a stately older woman dressed in fine fashion and glittering jewelry.

"Mother," said the son respectfully, "tell me his name."

"He is a very old man, but he still listens to the wind and walks with the maker of all. Sky can most assuredly tell you the meaning of these words."

So Sky was brought through the darkness to the palace. He was offered purple and gold and power if he could do what others could not.

"Keep your gifts," said Sky. "I will tell you the meaning.

"Dragon King learned the dangers of pride. He was driven from his people to eat the grasses of the fields among the wild animals. But your pride is greater than his, and you refuse to humble yourself as he did.

"You laugh at goodness.

"You drink from what is set apart.

"You curse the maker of all.

"Therefore the judgment of Heart-Lifter has been written. The words mean that you are unworthy to rule, so your reign will end immediately. Your resistance to Heart-Lifter and your attraction to Shining One have caused your fall. Before the sun rises, the Kingdom of the Bear will take the Kingdom of the Dragon."

The son of the king hid his face, for he knew in his heart that what was said was true. He looked into the eyes of Sky. "I know that my gifts will soon be meaningless, but I wish to honor you."

So the son clothed the old man in purple and hung a gold chain around his neck and made him the third ruler of his kingdom. The nobles applauded, but there was no joy. Soldiers of the Bear Kingdom had found a passage beneath the fortified walls. Before light appeared above the Mountains of the Dawn, sounds of battle were heard, and the guards were cut down. The enemy burst into the throne room. The nobles said nothing, and the son of the king did not move.

Bear King approached the young man and said, "I claim your kingdom and your life."

"I accept my fate," said the son.

Blood soaked the throne. The great Kingdom of the Dragon ended in silence and shame and darkness.

CHARACTER IS DEFINED
WHEN ONE'S DEEPEST BELIEFS
ARE CHALLENGED.

CHAPTER 4

THE DARK DEN

W̲ho is the wisest and most respected and most trustworthy man in all your kingdom?" Bear King asked the nobles of the kingdom he had overthrown. Without hesitation the nobles told him of Sky.

"It was Sky who foretold that you would destroy the Kingdom of the Dragon."

"Bring this man to me," Bear King ordered.

As the sun touched the Mountains of the Dawn, Sky walked with Heart-Lifter. "What shall I do?" he asked.

"Go to the royal palace and bow before Bear King. I will protect you and use your words to return my people to the City of Palms."

So Sky walked into the royal palace clothed in his purple robe, with a gold chain around his neck. The lines of nearly ninety summers marked his face, but his eyes were clear and his step straight.

"I am Sky," he said as he bowed before the king. "I have come to help you in any way you wish."

Bear King was surprised at the courage and confidence and calm of this elder statesman. The leaders and administrators of the bear wondered what their king would do. He had struck down the Dragon King by his own hand.

"How do you know what is unknown by others on the Blue Planet?" he demanded.

The old man looked directly into the king's eyes and spoke softly but firmly. "I listen to Heart-Lifter and his words are always true. It was he who. . .

"hung the sun above the clouds

"and separated land from sea

"and breathed life into the first man."

"And now you come to help the Kingdom of the Bear?" asked the king with a strange mixture of sarcasm and respect.

"I have come to do what Heart-Lifter tells me to do."

"The Kingdom of the Bear is now the largest country on the Blue Planet. I intend to choose three chief administrators to help me rule this great kingdom. Are you willing to be one of these administrators?"

"I am an old man," said Sky, "but if Heart-Lifter opens a door, I will not refuse to step through it."

Leaders of the Bear Kingdom looked at the gray-bearded man with disdain and jealousy, whispering among themselves, "This is not fair. How could our king place an outsider in such an important position? But he is old, and the work will soon wear him out."

But through the next year Sky did not wear out. Instead, he distinguished himself as the best among all the king's leaders. His wisdom and understanding and justice were so great that Bear King decided to set Sky as the chief administrator over all the kingdom, with authority exceeded only by his own.

Rumors spread quickly, and the other leaders knew that they would never become great in the kingdom until Sky was brought low. However, they could find nothing in his conduct or character to disqualify him from the high office. In all ways he was trustworthy and honorable and good.

"This outsider must be put in his place," said the most respected of the leaders.

"He is not one of us," said another. A snake slithered through the room with his twisted message of deceit and evil.

"Sky has one great weakness," said a tall man, hungry for power. "We can use it to trap him."

"What is his weakness?"

"Where and when can we use it?"

"How might we destroy him?"

"Sky clings to the ways of Heart-Lifter," said the tall man with a strange, serpentine smile. "So if he is trapped between the Bear King and the one who holds stars in his hands. . ."

"He will choose Heart-Lifter," agreed the leaders.

"Exactly," said the tall man.

So the leaders bowed low before their king. "We have agreed that your rule is still in danger until you prove that you are ultimate leader of this kingdom. Anyone who looks to another should be killed—thrown into the den of your lions. This order should be written on the legal scrolls and signed by your hand so it can be altered by no one."

"I see all my leaders standing before me except one," said the king. "Would Sky agree with this official order?"

"He is busy with his duties," said the tall man, "but he is one with us on the importance of such an order."

All the leaders nodded in guilty agreement.

"I will do as you think wise," said the king. "But I will only make such an order good for a single cycle of the moon. At that time, we will discuss whether the order shall stand."

The leaders agreed at once. Bear King had the order written on the legal scrolls and signed it with his own hand. Messengers proclaimed it throughout the kingdom.

The leaders knew that at the beginning and middle and end of each day, Sky would open a window of his house and look to Heart-Lifter, giving him honor and thanks and asking that his people be someday allowed to return to the City of Palms. They also knew that Sky would not stop this practice at the command of the king. They were right. Sky heard the royal order proclaimed in the streets and shook his head sadly. Then he went to his upper room and opened the windows and looked to the one above all. This time, however, enemies lay hidden, taking careful note of all they saw and heard.

"One of your leaders has ignored your command," the men said as they stood before the king. "Though you have given him favor, he has this day looked to someone besides you."

"The law stands as written for a single cycle of the moon. Who is this ungrateful rebel?"

"We regret that it is Sky himself. We have seen him go into his upper room and look to Heart-Lifter."

Bear King stood to his feet and shouted, "You told me that Sky agreed with this order!"

"We must have been mistaken."

"You deceived me. This law was based upon lies."

"But it was signed by your hand and cannot be altered," the leaders reminded the king.

"Leave me. I must consider this," said the king.

When the sun had descended into the west, the leaders stood once more before the king. "According to your order, Sky must be thrown into the den of royal lions. This law must be enforced before this day ends."

"What you say is true," admitted the Bear King. "Bring Sky before me."

Moments later, guards roughly pushed the old man into the throne room. The king looked on his close friend. "You know that in our kingdom not even the king can change a law. If I could, I would set you free. But instead you must go to the lions."

"I understand, my king," said Sky. "We both must do what is right. And Heart-Lifter is able to protect me, even from the teeth of hungry lions."

The guards dropped the prisoner through an opening in the roof of a cave where ferocious lions paced back and forth. The lions were given little food, and their hungry jaws were the terror that faced condemned criminals.

Sky hit the stone floor with a thud. When the covering was set over the opening, everything went black.

"You saved my friends from the heat of the fire, Heart-Lifter, and you are able to show this king your might. My life is in your care," cried Sky. He could not see the lions, but he could smell them as they growled and snarled and snapped. He felt the warm breath of one that sniffed him cautiously. The mighty beasts were circling, but they had not yet pounced and bitten into his trembling body. Sky knew Heart-Lifter was faithful, but the one above all does not always answer the way one might wish.

The lions moved closer.

Their growls grew louder.

They were moving in.

But then the dark den was bathed in brilliant light. Before the lions and the old man, an angel swung a flaming sword with his powerful arms. The lions cowered in a far corner.

"You are tired," said the angel. "Lay down and sleep in peace."

So Sky slept through the night. On the other side of the city, Bear King could not sleep. He was in anguish and knew that his friend had been brutally killed. He sat alone, refusing food and wine and pleasure. He stared at the walls and could find no peace.

At the first light of dawn, Bear King rushed to the lions' den. Guards removed the stone, and the king called down the small opening: "Sky? Do you live? Was Heart-Lifter great enough to save you?"

It took a few moments for the voice to rouse him. Sky rubbed his eyes and stretched his arms and stood to his feet. "I am alive. An angel has kept me from any harm. I have slept well, but the lions remain hungry."

The king ordered ropes to be thrown down, and Sky was lifted from the den. The king wrapped his arms around the old man.

"I have wronged you," said the king, "but I was deceived and signed a law that was not right. Now those who planned your ruin will take your place among the lions."

Every leader who had deceived the king was roused and bound and dragged protesting to the prison. Each was dropped screaming into the lions' den and caught in the beasts' jaws before he hit the floor.

Later the Bear King and Sky banqueted together. "I shall have an order written on the legal scrolls and signed by my own hand and proclaimed throughout my kingdom that Heart-Lifter is above all," said the king. "If there is ever anything you wish, come to me, and it shall be granted."

During the next cycle of the moon, Sky read the words that Weeping Prophet had written many years before. In a letter to the captives, he had said, "Live in this distant kingdom for seventy summers. Then Heart-Lifter will return you to your land."

Sky looked up dates
and scribbled notes
and calculated numbers.

It was true. The seventieth year from the time the first captives were taken away was not far off. In his graciousness, Heart-Lifter might begin to return the people even now. Sky poured out his heart to the one above all.

"Forgive your people for our foolishness. You gave us all, yet we were not satisfied. We did not look beyond the sky or listen to your words or walk in your ways. When you warned us, we did not humble our hearts. So you took our land and destroyed our city and scattered us to distant countries. Now set us free, so that we might return to the City of Palms and rebuild your sanctuary."

A gentle breeze blew through the room as twilight touched the land. "Walk with me," whispered the wind.

"You are Heart-Lifter, the infinite and eternal and all-powerful."

"Long ago, as Promise-Keeper, I led Merchant across the fertile crescent to the land you walked as a child. I still keep promises."

"May we return?"

"Look up. Tell me what you see."

"Stars. Thousands of brilliant stars."

"What is the promise of the stars?"

"No matter how dark the path, you will always show the way."

"That is my promise. Tomorrow when the morning brightens your windows, go to Bear King. He will let your people return."

The wind was gone, and the stars shone more brilliant than Sky could ever remember.

WHEN THOSE WITHOUT SCRUPLES
TEAR DOWN,
THOSE WITH FAITH AND COURAGE
MUST REBUILD.

THE REBUILDING

Y ou may return to your homeland, though I will miss your counsel," Bear King said to Sky.

"Thank you, great king. This tired old body cannot make such a journey, but some of my people do wish to return and rebuild their city. If you give your permission, I would be very happy."

"I will grant your request and even more. I will return the treasures that Dragon King took from the sanctuary to Heart-Lifter and provide the gold needed to rebuild it."

"You have given more than I thought possible," said Sky. "I have longed for this day all my life—to hear that the captivity of my people is nearly at an end, and they will be able to return to rebuild the Special Place in the City of Palms."

A proclamation was made throughout the kingdom: "Heart-Lifter has touched the heart of Bear King. Every captive from the land west of the Winding River is free to return to the highlands and settle in the City of Palms and rebuild the sanctuary of the one beyond the sky. The Kingdom of the Bear will open its treasury to assure completion of this project."

Most captives were unprepared for this proclamation, and many families had difficult decisions to make.

Some could hardly wait to go.

More did not want to leave their good homes.

Most felt the pull of both possibilities.

"I am the grandson of Winter King and heir to the throne of the People of the Promise," said a strong and handsome man. "Though I wear no crown and submit to the bear, I am your rightful leader."

People nodded in agreement, for they knew the grandson to be a man of honesty and wisdom and ability. In all, fifty thousand people were prepared to journey west across the fertile crescent. As the day of leaving approached, wagons were built and cattle collected and belongings packed. Those who stayed behind sent gifts with their returning family—silver and gold, food and clothing, livestock and jewelry.

The uncrowned grandson stood before the travelers and asked Sky to bless them.

"Heart-Lifter will be with you, but do not forget him," said Sky. "Do not be fearful or distracted or weary. Let nothing stop you from raising a sanctuary from the rubble."

"We shall do as you say," said Grandson.

"Heart-Lifter will send two encouragers with you," said Sky. "These encouragers will listen closely to him. One is old with the strong hands of a worker, and one is young with the deep devotion of a keeper. Both will be truth tellers and both will walk with the one who holds stars in his hands."

Sky placed his hands on the encouragers as they knelt before him. Then he said good-bye to his people.

Suddenly trumpets blew, and Bear King walked through the crowds to Grandson. Behind him came many servants carrying silver and gold.

"These were taken by Dragon King, some from the sanctuary, some from the palace, and some from the people of the City of Palms. Take them with you to help you rebuild your Special Place and your city and your dreams."

Excitement spread as Grandson led the captives over the Great River. After a hard trek across the fertile crescent, they touched the land claimed by Merchant so long before. But their countenances fell as they approached the brush and brambles that covered the rubble of their city. Scorpions and snakes lived in the ruins. Could this have been the unconquerable citadel of kings?

There were no walls,

no palace,

no sanctuary to Heart-Lifter.

It took work even to find where these structures had once stood.

The settlers cleared fields outside the city and planted crops. Then little by little, they reclaimed land within the city and built houses. They chased away the jackals and began to be a community in the desolate place.

After three cycles of the moon, those who had returned gathered before the place where the sanctuary had stood. Craftsmen had skillfully set large stones to form an altar. For the first time in seventy years, keepers of the sanctuary sacrificed offerings of spotless, newborn lambs. As the sweet smoke drifted beyond the sky, Heart-Lifter smiled upon his people.

That night a breeze blew brisk on Grandson's face. "The sacrifices touch my heart," said the one above all. "But do not forsake the rebuilding of the Special Place."

"We shall dedicate ourselves to the task," promised Grandson.

Stonemasons went south to quarry the best stones that could be found. Carpenters went north to find beautiful cedars within reach of the Great Sea. All this was authorized and paid for by Bear King. The sanctuary site was cleared of rubble and briars. Footings were dug and the first great foundation stones set into bedrock. When this was completed, the people celebrated with trumpets and cymbals and joy. There were some, however, who wept, old men and women who remembered the splendor of the past. This building could not compare with that built by Wise King. Its glory was much less than they had hoped. But at least something was rising from the ruins that had marked the spot for too long.

To the north, a people watched all this work with resentment. When the Northern Kingdom had fallen, nearly two hundred summers before, Bull King brought in captives from other countries to fill the fields and valleys and cities of this new conquest. When the Kingdom of the Bull fell, the people had freedom to do as they wished. Some claimed to follow Heart-Lifter, but not much was remembered about him. The people listened mainly to the words of Shining One. They sent leaders to Grandson with a proposal:

"If you must rebuild the Special Place, let us work side by side with you. Then we can bow before our maker together as brothers and offer spotless, newborn lambs as friends."

"The rebuilding is our responsibility," said Grandson. "Once it is finished, you may come to bow before our maker and offer your spotless, newborn lambs to the one above all."

The ambassadors went north in anger. They had thought to stop the rebuilding from within. Now they were determined to stop the work from outside.

They threatened.

They discouraged.

They sent delegates to Bear King.

"Stop the rebuilding of the sanctuary in the City of Palms," begged the delegates.

"I commanded that the sanctuary be rebuilt," said the king. "My word is law."

So work continued, ever so slowly. After six summers, Bear King died. Second King took his place. The resentful ones quickly sent another petition.

"The captives who returned to the City of Palms say they quarry rock and fell cedar for their sanctuary, but what they are really doing is restoring the great walls to stand against your soldiers when they rebel. Dragon King knew this, so he destroyed this treasonous city, tearing apart its walls. If you do not act to stop them, you will lose this part of your kingdom and be laughed at throughout the Blue Planet."

Second King was concerned about this report. Advisors confirmed that in the past, the City of Palms had been a strong and stubborn citadel— quick to revolt.

"Should I let this threat grow?" the king asked those whom he trusted most.

"No!" came the unanimous response.

"Then all rebuilding in the City of Palms must stop immediately," said Second King. His words were written on the royal scroll and signed with his own hand. Thus all work on the sanctuary ceased, and the people were discouraged.

One morning, many years later, the people assembled in the center of the City of Palms to hear the words of the encouragers.

"I am the Old Encourager," spoke the man with thin hair and poor eyes. "You have no one to blame but yourselves, for by now the Special Place should have been finished. And now, instead of working to rebuild the sanctuary, you enlarge your houses and panel rooms with fine cedar, which should go to please the one above all."

"Second King ordered us to stop," complained the people.

"But Heart-Lifter ordered us to start," said the elderly man. "To whom should we listen?"

"Humble your hearts and look to the sky," said the Young Encourager. "The maker of all is waiting."

"But we shall all be killed by the Army of the Bear," said a leader.

"Heart-Lifter is able to guard you," said the Old Encourager.

"Return to your task," said the younger.

Grandson and the chief keeper joined the two encouragers. "What these men say is right," said Grandson. "Even if no one else is willing to join us, today we four shall start rebuilding the Special Place."

The crowd gasped as the Uncrowned King and the chief keeper set aside their robes and began to work on the partially completed sanctuary. Soon stonemasons stepped forward to move a large stone into place. Then carpenters took out tools to shape and smooth the timbers. Soon most of those within the city crowded the building site to see what they could do.

Second King never heard of this action, for he died and Third King was crowned. The new king appointed leaders to oversee his kingdom, and one of these leaders heard about the building in the City of Palms. He journeyed to the ruined city and went to the sanctuary to ask questions.

"What are you doing?

"Who gave you permission?"

"How many are working on this?"

"We are doing what our maker told us to do," said Grandson. "We all work together and we all stand together."

Several hundred workers surrounded the man who was asking questions. He grew fearful and left the city without demanding the project to stop. When he was safely back at his home, he wrote to Third King.

"I recently journeyed to the City of Palms to assure that the law against rebuilding was obeyed. I found that the people were rebuilding their sanctuary. They were carving large stones and placing cedar timbers. They told me that Bear King had made a royal proclamation to rebuild the sanctuary at its original site. I know nothing of such a proclamation. But if what they say is true, they must complete this project. I suggest that the king order a search of the archives to see if such a proclamation exists."

Third King agreed. He ordered that the records be searched and found a tablet with a proclamation by Bear King. It confirmed what the people had said.

"If Bear King ordered the sanctuary rebuilt," said Third King, "then it shall be rebuilt. No one is to interfere. I shall open the royal treasury to provide gold needed to assure that the sanctuary is speedily completed. Anyone who attempts to stop the rebuilding in the City of Palms will die."

A scribe wrote down each word. The king signed his name and it was read throughout the land.

For nearly four more summers, the People of the Promise labored on the sanctuary. Men lifted timbers. Women wove curtains. Grandparents worked beside their grandchildren, each doing what he or she was able.

"Heart-Lifter will bless your diligence," said the Old Encourager.

"The one beyond the sky sees your obedience," said the Young Encourager. "He will make your crops bountiful and your vines fruitful and your cattle fat. He will regather his scattered people and again dwell among us."

The people completed the Special Place and put into place the treasures taken by Dragon King. Keepers stood before the sanctuary's altar to offer hundreds of spotless newborn lambs to the one above all. For seven days they feasted and sang and danced. On the seventh day they thanked Heart-Lifter for leading them back to their land and allowing them to rebuild the sanctuary.

That night the City of Palms slept more peacefully than it had in over a hundred summers, since Book King had repaired the sanctuary. Above the rooftops, brilliant stars reminded all who cared to look of the path back home.

Heart-Lifter smiled.

A POSITION OF AUTHORITY
CARRIES A GREAT BURDEN
OF RESPONSIBILITY.

CHAPTER 6

THE MAIDEN QUEEN

Third King looked east and built a magnificent winter palace in the Protected City at the foothills of the Mountains of the Dawn. It was the most beautiful palace ever built on the Blue Planet. High above the rest of the city, the grandeur of its size and architecture reminded all of the vast wealth of the Kingdom of the Bear.

When Third King died, his son wore the crown. He made Protected City his home and expanded the palace to even greater magnificence. His throne room had seventy-two fluted marble columns, each twelve times the height of a good-sized man. Its walls were of brick covered with glazed tiles brightly painted with bears and birds and unicorns, lilacs and lilies and roses. The palace was surrounded by enclosed gardens with animals and plants from throughout the known world.

The new king was tall and muscular and the most handsome man in his kingdom. He was a brave warrior, determined to expand his realm to the islands and inlets and northern shores of the Great Sea.

In the third year of his reign, Brave King held long strategic planning meetings for all the leaders and princes and nobles of his kingdom. They spent many days plotting to conquer the northern shores. Nearly two million men were enlisted as warriors and sailors and laborers. When all the plans were complete, Brave King held a grand banquet for every man in the city. A great pavilion was built in the royal gardens, large enough to keep ten thousand sheltered from the afternoon sun.

For seven days, silver platters were filled with the richest food of the land, and golden goblets were filled with the finest wine. The men told stories and played games and made challenges.

On the final day, Brave King had drunk many goblets of wine. "I am the most blessed man in all the Blue Planet," he shouted in a slurred speech, "and I have the most beautiful wife in all my kingdom.

"Her hair is exquisite.

"Her face is fair.

"Her form is shapely.

"If any of you saw her, you would have to agree that there lives no one more beautiful."

"Show her!" shouted back an officer who had drunk too much wine to realize his disrespect to the king and queen.

"Prove it!" shouted another.

The king called for his personal servants. "Tell my wife to come to dance before us in her golden crown and her most revealing gown. Tell her we must gaze upon her beauty and grace and shapeliness."

"He wants me to dance before ten thousand drunken strangers?" cried his wife when she heard the command. "I am a queen, not a dancing slave. How could he ask such a thing?"

"You must go," said the chief servant. "If you do not, the people will laugh at the king."

"Then he deserves to lose their respect."

"Not on the eve of war. It could be disastrous!"

"I will not go."

The chief servant finally went to Brave King, who threw his goblet on the ground and splattered banqueters far across the room. His face turned red, and he yelled incoherently.

The next morning, the king's memory of the previous night was unclear. He rubbed bloodshot eyes and splashed water on a swollen face. He sat silent and shamefaced as his advisors described his unfortunate actions.

The king sighed.

"I love my wife, and I was drunk and foolish. But she refused to obey a command of the king."

"According to the law, she should die," an advisor said. "You cannot lose the respect of your people as you undertake a great campaign."

"She need not die in such a case," disagreed the wisest advisor, "but you must take action, for she wronged you and all the nobles and people who trust you to be their strong, brave king. Also, many women admire the queen. If she can disregard her husband's authority, so can they. There will be no end to the trouble."

"So I must act quickly." said the king.

"The husbands of the kingdom depend on it."

"Then bring me my scroll and I shall make a royal decree," ordered the king.

"The queen shall never again enter my presence.

"She shall lose her position.

"Her place shall go to another."

The decree was written and signed by the king and proclaimed in every city. But Brave King needed a queen to produce an heir. He asked his nobles to search the kingdom for the most beautiful women. Four hundred maidens were selected, and each was carefully prepared for her presentation before Brave King.

In Protected City lived a prominent scribe of great integrity. His parents had been born in the City of Palms and had been captured by Dragon King. Though he was far away, he rejoiced at word that the sanctuary had been rebuilt. During the day the scribe worked in the palace. At night he looked to the sky, confident in the promise of the stars: No matter how dark the path, he will always show the way.

Scribe and his wife did not have a child of their own, but they took in the child of relatives who had died and raised the young girl as if she were their own daughter. Her name was Star, for she shined in face and form, in heart and soul and every aspect of her character. Star had seen fifteen summers when Brave King's proclamation was read on the street. Soon nobles took her to the palace to join the women who would be presented to the king. Within a cycle of the moon, Star won the favor of those who were over the young women, so they took extra care in training her to please the king and act as a queen.

All of the women were taught the royal ways.

They bathed in fragrant oils

and dressed in elegant clothing
and ate the finest foods.

When Brave King returned from his grand crusade, his heart was low, for he had failed to conquer the northern shores. He cheered as he met the four hundred. They were all attractive, but Star stood out. When Brave King looked at Star and spoke with her, his heart rose. During the winter and spring, Brave King's attraction for Star grew. She won his affection and favor and approval. So the king set a golden crown on her head, and she became his queen. He gave a banquet and proclaimed a holiday and gave gifts to every guest. All this for the love of his new bride.

Star kept her secret that she was of the People of the Promise and that her adopted father was a royal scribe. One day when Star came to visit Scribe, he had a very heavy heart.

"What is wrong?" Star asked when she saw the darkness in his eyes.

"I was sitting at the royal gate and heard two palace guards plot against the kingdom. They were angry and evil and determined to kill Brave King."

"I must tell my husband," said Star.

"Go quickly and tell him all you have heard."

Star ran to the king. The two guards were questioned and admitted their plan.

"Where did you hear of this plot?" asked the king.

"From Scribe who works faithfully in your palace," said Star.

"Tell him I owe him much for saving my life."

Three summers later, Brave King honored a desert prince and gave him a seat beside his throne with more power than all the other leaders of the Protected City. All the palace officials at the royal gate knelt before the desert prince and pledged their unwavering loyalty to him. But Scribe would neither kneel nor pledge.

"If you do not kneel, Desert Prince will be offended and your life will be in danger," said a group of concerned palace officials who came to Scribe.

"The only one to whom I kneel and pledge my unwavering authority is Heart-Lifter."

"But many of your people are willing to kneel to others if it keeps them from the gallows."

"I trust my life to the maker of all. He will be my protection," said Scribe. "The Desert People have been enemies of my people since the days of General. They despise the one who holds stars in his hands. I will not honor their leader."

Day after day the palace officials knelt, while Scribe stayed firmly on his feet. Desert Prince was enraged and ready to end the life of Scribe.

"Do you know why he shows such disrespect?" said a snake that followed the prince to his elegant home.

"I do not care why. I just want to see him hanging from the gallows."

"He walks with Heart-Lifter, and his family once lived in the City of Palms."

"I hate the People of Promise."

"And they hate you," said the snake with an evil sneer. "Many times they tried to destroy your people, but now you are in a position to destroy them."

The smile crossed from the ancient serpent to the Desert Prince.

An idea seriously considered.

A wicked plan perfected.

A strategy went to action.

When all was ready, Desert Prince went to Brave King. "There is danger in your kingdom. A people are scattered throughout your kingdom whose ways are different than yours. This group does not understand your beliefs and does not respect your authority and does not obey your commands. If something is not done, this difficult and defiant people will cause great trouble."

"What should be done?"

"Issue a decree that this people, every man and woman and child, should be destroyed."

"Write up such a decree," said the king, "and I shall place my name on it."

So Desert Prince wrote a decree that every individual, man and woman and child, born of the People of Promise should be killed. On a specific day shortly before winter turns to spring, as the sun first touches the Mountains of the Dawn, every warrior of the Kingdom of the Bear is to turn against these people with swords and spears and daggers. As a reward, each warrior shall plunder the goods of those he has killed.

The decree was signed and proclaimed in every city of the vast Kingdom of the Bear. As Desert Prince and Brave King drank together in the magnificent palace, the People of Promise reeled in shock at the proclamation.

When Scribe heard the decree, he wept and tore his clothes and refused to eat. He cried out, "Why is the king determined to destroy my people?"

Star's servants brought her news of Scribe's distress, and she sent food and clothing, but he would not accept them. She could not go to speak with him, and a person in mourning could not enter palace grounds. So she sent her most trusted servant to discover what troubled him.

"Desert Prince has tricked Brave King into signing a decree that will mean death to the People of Promise," said Scribe. "Take this to Star and read it to her." Scribe handed him a scroll that held a copy of the decree of destruction. "Then urge her to go humbly to the king, to plead for her people."

Star's servant told her all that Scribe had said and read to her the king's decree. Star quickly sent back her reply.

"I wish to plead for my people, but anyone who approaches the king in his inner court without being summoned will be put to death. He has not summoned me for many days. Only if he extends his golden scepter to me will my life be spared."

A reply came within an hour: "If you do not approach the king, you and your family and your people will die. Heart-Lifter places people like you in positions of power to fulfill just such tasks."

"Go gather all the People of Promise in the Protected City," came Star's response. "Tell them to neither eat nor drink for three days. They must look beyond the sky and cry out to the maker of all to soften the king's heart. On the third day. . .

"I will place my life in Heart-Lifter's hands.

"I will approach the king.

"If I perish, I perish."

The People of Promise did as Star requested.

CHAPTER 7

THE SAVING

All the People of Promise who lived in the vast lands of the Kingdom of the Bear were in grave danger. Desert Prince had become one of the most influential rulers and advisors to Brave King, and he was a most bitter enemy of Heart-Lifter and his people. Desert Prince was descended from a people who had hated and harassed and battled the people of Heart-Lifter since the days of General, when the nation first crossed the desert to claim what the one above all had promised to give them. Now the people were under the rule of Brave King, and he had been tricked by Desert Prince into signing an irrevocable law. On a certain day, at about the time the winter was turning to spring, all the People of Promise could be hunted down and destroyed. Desert Prince had planned his attack well, but he could not have figured on one thing. Brave King's own beloved bride, Maiden Queen, was one of those whose destruction had been ordered. To save her people, Maiden Queen decided to take a desperate gamble. She would approach the king unbidden. To do so normally meant death—unless the king extended his scepter to allow the petitioner to approach.

After three days during which the people of Heart-Lifter called upon the one who is above all, Star bathed in fragrant oils and put on her royal robes and placed her golden crown on her elegantly braided hair. She stood outside the inner court of the palace.

Her hands shook.

Her heart trembled.

Her mind raced.

She looked beyond the sky and asked Heart-Lifter to walk close beside her. Then she stepped into the inner court and moved slowly, respectfully toward her husband, who sat facing her on his royal throne. She felt very small and insignificant as she passed the massive fluted columns. The wall tiles sparkled in the morning sun, making Star squint as she continued forward. Those in the room looked on in silent fear, tinged with admiration, for the courageous young woman. Her petition must be of the utmost importance. Brave King's face betrayed no expression as he set down the document he had been studying and watched her approach.

"Maiden Queen." The king's gentle, loving voice echoed through the hall, and the people breathed normally once more. "What may I do for you?"

Star stopped and said nothing. Brave King smiled, but he had not yet extended the golden scepter to her. He finally realized the problem and extended it. Maiden Queen's sigh of relief was part of a collective exhale among the people who were standing by.

"What do you wish?" the king asked once more.

"If it pleases you," she said, "would the king and Desert Prince come to a private dinner I have prepared?" Everyone looked at her quizzically, for Maiden Queen had braved death for such a simple request. But the king showed no sign of surprise.

"We will come."

Brave King and Desert Prince reclined at Star's elegant dinner. As they drank wine from golden goblets, the king again asked: "What do you wish? Anything you desire, up to half the kingdom, shall be yours."

Star smiled sweetly and kneeled by her husband and took his hand. "If I have won your affection and favor and approval, come to another dinner I have prepared for tomorrow afternoon. Bring Desert Prince. I will tell you then what I wish."

Desert Prince walked toward his home that night in high spirits. Passing through the royal gate, all the palace officials knelt before him—all except Scribe. Even this could not ruin Desert Prince's day. He would, after all, soon see this brazen man and his relatives slaughtered.

That evening Desert Prince gathered together his friends and family at his impressive house near the city wall. "Maiden Queen invited me to join Brave King at her private dinner this afternoon. We are to return for another dinner tomorrow."

His friends and family were duly impressed. "All of this would be wonderful, if it were not for Scribe and his refusal to show me my proper respect." He told them that, once again, the people had all bowed before him except for Scribe.

"He mocks you," said his bitter wife.

"Scribe deserves to be punished," said one of his sons.

"He deserves to die," said his wife.

"Why don't you have a high gallows built," said another son, "and ask the king to hang Scribe on it so all can see?"

It was such a satisfying thought. Yes, he would order the gallows built at once, and the king would allow him to do as he wished with his enemy. He called for his sons to summon workmen and start construction immediately.

Late that same night, as the gallows on which Scribe was to hang were being assembled, Brave King also paced the floor, for he could not sleep. The room was too hot, and he had eaten too much the day before. And there was one thing more. He felt he had forgotten something—something important. He paced the room awhile longer. But whatever it was he wished to recall would not come to his memory.

He ordered his servants to bring him the royal scrolls of his reign.

"Read them to me," he said. "Start at my first year and read every word."

The servants did as they were told. All night long they read of events that had happened and problems brought to the king's attention and decisions he had made. Suddenly, as the sun rose above the Mountains of the Dawn, the king stopped them.

"You have just read to me about the plot on my life. I remember how Scribe warned Maiden Queen of the danger. Scribe saved me and the kingdom. What honor has Scribe received for his loyalty?"

"Nothing has been done for him."

A servant entered the room. "Desert Prince asks to see you."

"Bring him in," said the king absently, as he thought about a reward for Scribe.

"Advise me, my friend," said the king when Desert Prince stood before him. "Someone has shown great loyalty to the kingdom. How should I show my high regard for him?"

Desert Prince could not believe his good fortune. Surely it was he himself who was being singled out for immense honor, and now the king was asking what that honor should be.

"Give this deserving man your finest royal robe.

"Place him upon your grandest stallion.

"Have a noble lead him through the city shouting, 'This is a man in whom the king delights!'"

"An excellent idea!" said Brave King. "Go at once to Scribe who sits by the royal gate. Give him my robe and place him upon my stallion and lead him through my city as you suggested."

Desert Prince was horrified, but he had no choice but to do as the king ordered. Afterward he rushed home in humiliation.

"Be careful," said his wife when she heard. "Your plans to punish Scribe may be about to turn on you."

Later a chastened Desert Prince joined the king for the private dinner set out by Star. As they drank wine from golden goblets, the king asked his Maiden Queen once more, "What do you wish? Ask anything, up to half the kingdom, and it shall be yours."

"If I have won your affection and favor and approval," Star said softly as she knelt by her husband, "please spare my life and the lives of my people."

Confusion darkened the king's face. "Who in my kingdom has dared to threaten my precious queen?"

Through her tears, Star pointed at the mystified Desert Prince. "This man plots to kill my family and many more. He wrote the decree to have the People of Promise destroyed. It has been signed and proclaimed throughout the kingdom. I am one of those whose death was ordered."

Desert Prince's heart fell.

His face turned pale.

His tongue grew thick and twisted.

Brave King rose in anger and faced Desert Prince. "You deceived me?"

he shouted at Desert Prince. In his rage, he burst through the side doors into the palace gardens to walk and think and consider what to do.

Desert Prince bowed low before the queen and then grasped her hand.

"I did not know!" he cried. "I never meant you harm."

Star tried to pull away, but Desert Prince clung tightly in fear.

She pulled back quickly, throwing him off balance. He grabbed her shoulders to brace himself, but they toppled onto the couch. She screamed and her husband rushed into the room.

Desert Prince scrambled to his feet with a guilty look upon his face.

"You attack my wife legally and then you attack her physically. Before the sun sets, you shall die."

"Dear king," said a servant, "Desert Prince has erected a high gallows on which to hang Scribe in the marketplace."

"Hang Desert Prince on it," ordered the king.

Guards dragged him away.

"Thank you for saving Scribe, who has been as a father to me," said Star.

"All the power and position and possessions that once belonged to Desert Prince shall now belong to Scribe," declared the king.

Star fell at his feet and wept and thanked him. "There is one more thing," she said, looking up at him. "What can be done to stop Desert Prince's decree?"

"It cannot be rescinded," admitted the king darkly. "But perhaps Scribe knows what decree can be quickly put into motion that might save your people."

Soon heralds were running to every part of the kingdom to read a new law: "On the day when the winter is turning to summer that the People of Promise are attacked, each man is to arm himself. Let him strike down those who would harm him and his family. On this day and even on the next day they may gather together to destroy all who have raised a hand against them."

Scribe entered the impressive throne room with its seventy-two fluted marble columns. The king placed a blue and white robe of the finest linen upon his shoulders, and Protected City celebrated. Throughout the land, the People of Promise. . .

sang in happiness,

danced in joy,

and feasted in thanksgiving.

Scribe's decree gave them hope and confidence and strength. They gathered to sharpen their weapons. Even people of other nations stood with them as brothers.

So on the day Desert Prince had set, warriors went out as the sun rose above the Mountains of the Dawn. But when they came upon the People of Promise, who had gathered on battlefields of their own choosing, the people were well able to defend themselves. In every city there was an attack, and in every city the attackers were turned back. No one could stand against those who looked to Heart-Lifter.

At the end of the day, Star thanked her husband for supporting her people.

The followers of Heart-Lifter cheered at their victory. Music and dancing and feasting filled every city in the kingdom.

Scribe recorded all these events and sent letters to the People of Promise throughout the Blue Planet. He called them to set aside this day as the day of their saving, from this year forward.

"It shall be our reminder of a time when enemies were defeated and sorrow turned to joy and mourning became celebration. This day shall be remembered with every generation by every family in every city."

And so it was. Star, the Maiden Queen, left a legacy that would never be forgotten.

EMBRACING TRUTH
MAY INVOLVE A RISK.
BUT NOT EMBRACING TRUTH
INVOLVES A GREATER RISK.

CHAPTER 8

THE TEACHER

You know more about the People of Promise than any other on the Blue Planet," said the aged government official called Scribe.

"Heart-Lifter has been good to me," said Teacher.

"I would like you to move to the Summer Palace in the City of Stars and be the spokesman for our people," explained Scribe.

"I will go where Heart-Lifter wants me to go," said Teacher.

Teacher was a man of some thirty years, with strong convictions and a sharp mind. He was a scholar and writer whose firm fingers were stained with dark ink. On scrolls he had written the words of the Book of King-doms, and now he was writing about Grandson and the rebuilding of the sanctuary.

Teacher was descended from General's brother. He had neither wife nor children, for most of his time was spent teaching and writing and pointing his people to the one beyond the sky.

Scribe had poured all he knew into Teacher as a spiritual father and friend and guide. So when Scribe offered him the royal position, Teacher was both honored at the opportunity and unhappy at leaving his mentor.

Teacher rose before the sun. He walked the foothills of the Mountains of the Dawn in the half-light, half-sleep moments that yearn for morning, yet cling to night. Teacher followed Heart-Lifter along footpaths and through meadows. As the sun sparkled on dew-drenched wildflowers, he was far from Protected City. He climbed a steep hill. Teacher perspired and slowed and sighed, but he did not stop. By midmorning he stood atop a mighty hill and looked west across a stunning panorama. Teacher had walked farther than he had ever traveled before. But he did not comment or complain, he simply followed the one who holds stars in his hands.

"Do you love me?" said the wind.

"I love you with all my heart," said Teacher as he gasped to catch his breath after the vigorous climb.

"Do you trust me?" said the wind.

"With all my life."

"Will you do whatever I ask?"

Teacher knew what the answer should be and he yearned to say "yes" without hesitation, but his throat would not make a sound. He knew what Heart-Lifter was about to ask. It seemed too hard.

His maker was about to ask him to leave his home and his scrolls and his dearest friend. He loved the Protected City and his familiar routine. Teacher did not care for risk or change, but he was on the brink of both.

Teacher fought back his tears. He faced the wind with a determination to do what was good and right and honorable.

"Yes," he said with a strength of choice. "I will do whatever you ask."

"Go west," said the wind. "Go first to the City of Stars and then beyond. Go west like Merchant and Seer and Grandson."

"Today I will pack my belongings."

The next day Teacher said good-bye to Brave King and Maiden Queen. He hugged Scribe and left the city of his birth.

In the City of Stars, Teacher took up a high position in the summer palace, where he served the Kingdom of the Bear and the People of Promise as best he could.

During the next few years, Brave King and Scribe passed from the Blue Planet. Both men were greatly mourned and sorely missed. Brave King's oldest son was crowned, and he moved his home to the City of Stars. This young king was a kind and generous man who soon befriended Teacher.

Seven years passed. Early one morning, as the sun touched the Mountains of the Dawn, Teacher walked with Heart-Lifter.

"Do you love me?" asked the wind.

"With all my heart."

"Do you trust me?"

"With all my life."

"Will you do whatever I ask?"

"Yes," he said with both strength and confidence.

"Go west," said the wind. "Go west to the City of Palms. Take with you whoever wishes to return to their homeland. Go to my sanctuary and point my people beyond the sky and sacrifice spotless, newborn lambs on the stone altar before the Special Place."

Teacher shared the words of Heart-Lifter with those within the city, and people gathered around him. They listened to every word, for they held this man in great respect.

His people respected his wisdom.

The kingdom respected his knowledge.

Generous King respected his character.

Within a week Teacher was called to the throne room. "I have heard your words," said the king. "Why does Heart-Lifter want you to go to the City of Palms?"

"The sanctuary was rebuilt nearly sixty summers ago, but its keepers have not done what they should. They have not pointed the people beyond the sky or taught them the words of their maker. I must go to help my people walk with Heart-Lifter."

"What you say is important," said the king. "I wish to send you to the City of Palms to do what Heart-Lifter asks. Whoever wishes may go. I give you silver and gold to buy spotless, newborn lambs. Please sacrifice these in my name on the altar before the sanctuary. If you have need of more silver or gold to fulfill the wishes of the maker of all, go to any treasury within the Kingdom of the Bear and what you ask for shall be yours.

"I ask one thing more," said Generous King. "Bring order to your people. Teach them justice and right from wrong and the foolishness of evil."

"I shall do as you say."

"And I shall have all these words written and proclaimed throughout the land."

Soon those who wished to travel gathered by the canal north of the City of Stars. Slowly, wagons packed high and heavy with possessions rolled in.

A hundred families.

A thousand families.

A thousand and five hundred.

That night the meadows were ablaze with campfires, as people sang and danced. Excitement was everywhere. They were going to the land of their ancestors and the city of their kings.

"Look up," said Teacher.

The people looked and said, "We see stars."

"Yes," said Teacher. "Heart-Lifter has given the stars to remind us of his promise."

The next day Teacher told the travelers to refrain from food and look beyond the sky and ask for the hand of Heart-Lifter to guard their journey.

"The road to our homeland has bandits and raiders and enemies," said Teacher, "but we need not fear, for the one who holds stars in his hands is our sword and shield and protector."

Several days later the People of Promise formed a great caravan of wagons and camels and livestock. In the center of the caravan was the silver and gold that Generous King had given—thirty wagons of pure silver and three wagons of fine gold. Rumors spread throughout the fertile crescent of the great wealth that was being carried from the City of Stars to the City of Palms. There were no soldiers, no guards, no horsemen.

For five cycles of the moon, the People of Promise journeyed toward their homeland, and during this time the hand of Heart-Lifter was on the caravan.

No one was harmed.

No silver was taken.

No raid was successful.

Those of the city greeted their brothers and sisters, welcoming them home with cheers and songs and a thousand open arms. Teacher led his travelers directly to the sanctuary, where they all fell to their knees and looked beyond the sky and thanked their maker for the safe journey.

During the next cycles of the moon, Teacher stood before all the people of the city. He pointed them beyond the sky and taught the words of the maker and showed them how to walk with Heart-Lifter.

Early one morning, a crowd from the city approached Teacher. "We have done wrong," said the people. "We have married the daughters of Shining One. In loneliness and impatience we took women who did not look to the one who holds stars in his hands—fair maidens of the plains and deserts and pyramids. We have been unfaithful."

Teacher looked at the crowd with sadness, but he did not say a word. When they were finished, he tore his tunic and pulled hair from his head and fell to the ground. For seven hours he sat silent in the city square as the sun beat down and the dust settled on his shoulders. The crowd trembled at Teacher's silence, and waited.

As the sun sank toward the Great Sea, the man with the torn tunic moved. The crowd gasped. On his knees, Teacher raised hands to the sky and cried out.

"We have failed and we beg for mercy. You have given much, and there is no way we can repay all we have received. Please forgive us, for. . .

"we have not looked on your face,

"we have not listened to your words,

"we have not walked by your side.

"Many summers ago you told us not to marry the women of the land. But the People of Promise have taken as wives those whom you told them to leave alone. We bow in guilt and sorrow and repentance. Please forgive us and clean us and restore us to the place from which we have fallen."

Tears flowed from Teacher's eyes and dropped quietly to the dry, sandy soil before his knees. The people circled Teacher and wept bitterly. They too went to their knees and they repeated the words they had heard. "We have failed and we beg for mercy."

Then they turned to Teacher. "We wish to do what is good and right and honorable. We shall send every woman who follows Shining One back to the land of her birth, and we promise to never again marry those whom our maker has warned us to avoid."

Teacher rose to look into the eyes of the crowd. "Do you realize the difficulty of what you have promised?"

"Yes, but we are willing to do whatever Heart-Lifter asks," said the people.

"So you shall send your wives from this land and back to their people?"

"Yes," said the crowd in one voice.

"So be it," said Teacher. "And I will eat no food and drink no water until your promise is proclaimed to all those who dwell in the New Land."

The promise was proclaimed.

The women were sent away.

The people looked beyond the sky.

Twelve summers passed, in which Teacher taught and the people listened. But one day, a respected nobleman came to Teacher.

"My heart is greatly troubled," he said. "Please send me to my brother in the Protected City, for he can help us."

"What help can he provide?" asked Teacher.

"The City of Palms and its people are vulnerable to the enemies of Heart-Lifter. The stone walls of our city have never been rebuilt. We need help from Generous King, and my brother is very close to the king."

So Teacher sent a delegation to Protected City to inform the nobleman's brother. The brother was a trusted advisor in the Kingdom of the Bear. He was loyal to Generous King and he loved the People of Promise.

The road-weary delegation stood before the brother in the outer court of the Winter Palace. "We come as your humble servants from the City of Palms. Some 150 summers ago the walls were broken down and the gates were burned and the city was left defenseless. Since then the sanctuary was rebuilt and the sacrifices have been restored, but our city is still defenseless. Help us."

The nobleman's brother wept. "How could we have neglected this for so long?"

"We have been foolish," said the delegation. "But we wish to correct our wrong. Will you take our need to Generous King?"

For the next days, the nobleman's brother mourned and fasted and looked beyond the sky.

"Oh, holder of the stars," he cried, "listen to my weeping words and prepare my way so that Generous King will receive my request with favor. Let me be a Wall Builder in the City of Palms.

"Let me raise a great wall
"and hang strong gates
"and bring safety to the city."

A wind swept in from the desert and surrounded the brother. "I have heard your words and I shall heal your heart," said the wind. "You shall be my Wall Builder."

A song filled his heart as he looked west, toward the Great Sea and the City of Palms.

Far in the distance a colorful arch stretched across the sky. Wall Builder remembered the ancient promise: I am always close and I will always care.

THERE ARE MANY REASONS
TO LET RUBBLE LIE;
THERE ARE MANY MORE
TO REBUILD.

CHAPTER 9

THE WALL BUILDER

W hy are you sad?" asked Generous King when his servant and protector and friend came before the throne.

"Forgive my downcast eyes, but my heart is broken," said the servant. "I have heard news of the city of my ancestors, far away. The people there are desperate, for their walls lie ruined and the gates burned and they stand vulnerable before their enemies."

"Then I cry with you, my friend, for this is hard news. What would you have me do?"

The servant looked into the king's eyes. "I believe I could raise up my kinsmen and restore the walls. Please send me to the City of Palms."

"You are an able leader. But the task may be greater than you know. What do you need?"

"Yes, the task may be great indeed, and there are dangers on the road even getting to the Land of Promise. May I have horsemen and warriors to escort me? And may I have access to your forests in that land, to cut the beams for the city's gates and the wall's reinforcement?"

"Go and build in my name."

The journey across the fertile crescent took three cycles of the moon on a steady donkey. Horsemen led the way, and warriors walked beside the trusted advisor. When he saw the City of Palms in the distance, the man dismounted and knelt in the road and wept. Already he could see that this was a rural village, not the great citadel of centuries past. The only thing that gave hope was the sanctuary, standing tall amid the humble houses.

But surrounding the city were piles of broken rock and ruin and refuse. He wiped his eyes and resolutely mounted his donkey.

Teacher and a small group of noblemen met the company of warriors at what had once been the northern gate. "We welcome you to the ancient capital of the People of Promise."

"It is not worthy of the name," said the stranger.

"It is all we have," said Teacher.

"We shall see."

The important stranger was congenial but had little to say about why he had come. On the third night of his stay, he and a few of his guards secretly left the city through what had once been the western gate. By the glow of a torch he made his way around the city, studying the ruined wall. All he found were piles of stone, not one upon another.

Early the next morning, Wall Builder summoned the city leaders. "We are in great trouble," he began.

"Our walls are broken.

"Our gates are burned.

"Our protection is gone."

All this they knew, so they waited expectantly for the man to continue.

"Far away at Protected City, Heart-Lifter called me to this place to rebuild what lies in ruin."

"At last! Heart-Lifter has brought to us a Wall Builder," said the leaders. "Show us what to do." And immediately they began organizing the work.

Outsiders visiting the city soon noticed the clearing and the leveling and the reshaping of stones.

"What are you doing?" they asked.

Wall Builder regarded them coldly. "We are working so that this place can once more be a city worthy of praise as in days of old."

"You think you can turn piles of rubble into defense and respect," laughed the outsiders. "You have neither the back nor the ability nor the perseverance to complete such a task. The king will soon come to tear it down again."

"We build in the name of the king—and in the name of the one who holds stars in his hands," said Wall Builder.

The outsiders spit on the stones. They mocked and scorned and ridiculed all who labored beneath the hot, sweltering sun. But they were worried, for a defenseless city was at their mercy, but a wall might make these people harder to bully.

Wall Builder knew their thoughts. The next day he gathered all the men of the city before the sanctuary. He divided them into work groups, each with a section of wall to build. The workers took pride in their own sections, and each group worked hard. The foundations were finished, and the stones began to rise.

Soon the governor of the central highlands heard of the progress. He screamed at all about him.

"This is ridiculous!

"The wall is rubble!

"It can never be rebuilt!"

All agreed that the project was hopeless, and the workers were fools. Spies were sent to taunt the builders, but the work would not stop.

Stone upon stone. It was hard and heavy work.

Stone upon stone. With aching arms and sweating brows, the men labored.

Stone upon stone. The wall reached upward until it was nearly half the height of what it had been.

"How have they done so much in so little time?" shouted the governor.

"They worked with a will," said one of his spies. "They have closed the gaps and increased the wall and replaced the gates."

"We must stop this," the governor said. "We must march against the city and end the work. All must be dead so the great king does not hear of it."

Reports reached Wall Builder: "Many stand against you. They are marching south."

Wall Builder stood before the workers and said, "Do not fear, for Heart-Lifter is great and awesome."

He armed workers behind the lowest parts of the wall. He gave them swords and spears and bows. At each section he told them,

"Fight for your brothers,

"your sons and daughters,

"your wives and homes."

The governor of the highlands did not expect to attack a city that was ready for battle. His army waited and watched for an opportunity to tear down the wall. But the workers neither let down their guard nor slowed their efforts. With swords at their sides and stones in their hands, they built the wall higher.

The governor learned that the wall was solid and strong and growing taller.

"Why has our army not attacked?"

"Half of their men hold swords from first light of dawn until the stars claim the sky. The other half build."

"Attack at night."

"All the people from the surrounding countryside have moved into the city. Those who do not work by day stand guard by night."

"Call my army home," said the governor. "We shall find another strategy."

Days later a runner came to Wall Builder with a message from the governor: "Come, let us meet in the lowlands near the Great Sea. There we can talk of how we might live together peacefully."

Wall Builder laughed. "Do they think I cannot see their trap?" He sent the runner back with his answer: "I am directing a great project, and I cannot leave until all is finished."

Four times the governor's runners came. Four times Wall Builder declined the invitation.

Next, runners brought a personal letter from the governor.

"There is a rumor among the nations that you are building your city wall so that you might rebel against the Kingdom of the Bear. I have also heard that you are to be crowned king of your people. If you refuse to meet with me, I will be forced to report all I know to Generous King."

Wall Builder set down the letter and picked up his stylus to answer: "None of what you write is true, and you know it. Stop trying to intimidate us.

"I will not leave this city.

"I will not stop building.

"I will not be afraid."

Wall Builder returned to the wall, and the People of Promise worked even harder until all was done. From start to finish the wall was rebuilt in less than two cycles of the moon. When the last stone was put into place and all the gates properly secured, a cheer echoed off the surrounding hills. As nearby nations heard the news, their eyes were opened and their hearts fearful and their confidence shaken.

Several days later the People of Promise gathered near the eastern gate. On a high wooden platform stood their leaders.

An old man with a curly gray beard walked slowly to a heavy wooden table at the front of the platform. Everybody was silent. Teacher fingered a thick parchment scroll that rested on the table and moved his eyes close so his weak eyes could discern the all-important words. Teacher cleared his throat and smiled.

"Hear and understand the ten words that Heart-Lifter gave to General on the mountain."

Everyone stood in respect.

All leaned forward to hear and understand.

They looked beyond the sky.

From first light until the blazing sun stood straight overhead, Teacher read the scroll. He made each sentence clear and gave it meaning and drove it deep into the hearts of all who heard.

Tears ran freely down every face. The sobs of ten thousand ashamed people swept the city.

"We have rebelled against Heart-Lifter," said Teacher, "but do not mourn or grieve or weep, for our maker forgives. This is a day of celebration, for you have heard the words of the one who holds the stars in his hands."

So the people went forth and ate and drank. They sang and danced and thanked Heart-Lifter.

He had given them back their city.

He had helped them rebuild the wall.

He was infinite and eternal and all-powerful.

Day after day, for a cycle of the moon, the people returned to the wooden platform at the eastern gate and listened to Teacher. After these days of celebration, the people fasted and tore their clothes and confessed their failings.

The keepers of the sanctuary cried to the one beyond the sky.

"You made the Blue Planet and placed Man in the most beautiful of all gardens. You told Builder to make a boat. You called Merchant to the new land and protected Dreamer when he was sold into the Land of Pyramids. You strengthened General and Brother as they led your people out of the country of Delta King. You guided Point Man back to the new land and established Shepherd as king.

"But your people did not look to the sky or listen to your words or walk with you. Therefore the kingdom was split, and the north was captured and the south fell. We have returned to the land and never again shall we turn our backs on you."

All the People of Promise responded in confident unison.

"His words are our words.

"His work is our work.

"His ways are our ways."

As the sun slipped below the horizon, the sweet smoke of a thousand spotless, newborn lambs rose above the city walls and mingled with the stars before drifting beyond the sky. Heart-Lifter smiled, and on that night the stars sparkled with added brightness.

The keepers pointed upward and said, "Never forget the promise of the stars: No matter how dark the path, he will always show the way."

Trumpets blared atop the city walls, and two great choirs of singers broke forth in songs of joy. One stood on the eastern wall and the other on the western wall. Songs of thanksgiving answered one another, punctuated by cymbals and harps and lyres.

All night the celebration continued, and for the first time in many summers, the People of Promise felt the eternal truth of their name.

IT IS BETTER TO DIE
FOR WHAT IS RIGHT
THAN TO LIVE
FOR WHAT IS WRONG.

CHAPTER 10

THE CONQUEROR AND THE MADMAN

Since it had first become a kingdom, the leopard had stretched its muscles toward the rising sun. Slowly its influence spread across the islands and inlets and northern shores of the Great Sea. Since the days of Brave King and Maiden Queen, the Kingdom of the Bear had been preoccupied with holding back the leopard.

Now six kings had come and gone.

The world was changing.

Old powers would soon pass to new.

"Leopard King is about to invade our kingdom," said the runner. "He has gathered soldiers who will follow their king anywhere, and his eye is on you."

"The fool!" laughed Last Bear King. "We are the wealthiest kingdom on the Blue Planet. Doesn't he know that we are invincible?"

"But they are determined."

"What will happen if this ambitious king dies?" asked Last Bear King. "Who will lead then?"

"The king's son will surely take the throne. He is young and inexperienced and poses no threat."

"Then let us kill their king."

A conspiracy was formed, and the ruler of the Kingdom of the Leopard was murdered, and his son wore the crown. This young man of twenty summers was lean and courageous and disciplined. His face was clean shaven with a white and ruddy complexion. Though he was young, he was not easily forgotten, for none could withstand his intense, melting gaze.

Though he lacked in experience,
he was a trained strategist
and a skilled archer
and a fearless hunter.

He had been tutored by one of the greatest philosophers. Now two desires shaped an obsession. First, he loved the cry of battle. Second, he hated those who had killed his father.

He united his kingdom and expanded its borders. He marched north and south. When he was ready, he turned east toward the Kingdom of the Bear with tireless, battle-hardened warriors and swift horsemen and cunning new ideas about warfare. The Army of the Bear might have three times his number, but he was the conqueror.

When the Army of the Bear charged, they could not break the tight ranks of troops. They did not understand the new battle tactics, and when they were most confused, the conqueror charged and overwhelmed them.

For over a year the Army of the Leopard marched east, claiming every valley and river and city. Six days west of the City of the Crossroads, the leopard and the bear met once again. The Great Conqueror again claimed the field by his unusual tactics, and Last Bear King fled for his life among his warriors. Instead of pursuing, the Army of the Leopard turned south to take the City of Caravans and the City of Palms. The People of Promise surrendered peacefully and were treated with respect. Then Great Conqueror continued south to claim the Land of Pyramids. Last Bear King sent delegates to Great Conqueror to negotiate peace—

Bear King would give large portions of his best land
and immense sums of silver and gold
and even his daughter in marriage.

Nothing appeased the leopard. The Great Conqueror marched across the fertile crescent and met the remaining forces of his enemy on a plain not far from the City of Blood. For the third time the Leopard Army withstood the bowmen and the charges of their enemy. They then moved in to finish their foe. Last Bear King fled across the Mountains of the Dawn and his army fell apart. Humiliated by the cowardice of their leader, his generals entered the tent of Last Bear King late one night and took his breath.

Great Conqueror took the City of Stars and then Protected City. He plundered the Winter Palace of the Last Bear King, but he took nothing from the people. Then he marched east across the Mountains of the Dawn to conquer more kingdoms. Years later he returned to the City of Stars and married the daughter of Last Bear King.

By now Great Conqueror had the largest empire that had ever stood on the Blue Planet. He had everything he had ever wished, but he was not happy. He always had listened to the lies of Shining One. He had tested them and found them untrue, but instead of looking beyond the sky, he listened to more lies.

"You are weary after twelve summers of battle," said the snake. "Drink wine until your heart is calm and your spirit is bright and your body rests in the joy of dreamless sleep."

So Great Conqueror drank. Weakened by drunkenness, his body could not withstand a fever that raged through his body. On the eleventh morning of his sickness, he was dead.

Since the Great Conqueror had no heir to take the throne, his vast kingdom was split among his three most powerful generals. And the world went on. There were times of war and times of peace, but the influence of the leopard was never lost upon the Land of Promise. Life was hard, but it was tolerable until the coming of Madman.

Madman was descended from one of the three generals. He ruled over the eastern shores of the Great Sea. He was known for his great intellect, but also for a sickness and absurdity of mind. He was the most generous and the most cruel, refined yet given to gross debauchery. He studied the Land of Promise and saw both its strategic location and its unexploited natural wealth. So his rule became harsh. He demanded a third of all the grain harvest and half of all the fruit. With his wealth he launched an invasion of the Land of Pyramids and added that great realm to his kingdom. On his way home, he stopped at the City of Palms to loot the Special Place of its silver and gold.

He killed any who tried to stop him.

He spoke with arrogance.

He forbid any to look beyond the sky.

Madman placed his own advisors and officials over the City of Palms, demanding that the People of Promise abandon their traditions and submit to the ways of the leopard. Outwardly the people submitted. But a rebellion grew deep in many hearts. In secret the keepers sacrificed many spotless, newborn lambs to the one above all. They looked beyond the sky and asked for a deliverer.

It was the Land of Pyramids that first rebelled. Madman led a strong force into the deltas. This time Madman lost battles, and rumors spread to the City of Palms that he had fallen. The People of Promise rejoiced. The chief keeper of the sanctuary armed a thousand warriors and reclaimed the City of Palms for Heart-Lifter! He killed every advisor and official who served Madman.

But Madman was not dead, and he turned back toward the City of Palms in fury. He retook the sacred city with the slaughter of many men and women and children.

Madman plundered the city
and put it to the flames
and tore down its mighty wall.

Madman entered the Special Place, stripping it of its remaining silver and gold. He assembled the people before the sanctuary. "This place no longer belongs to Heart-Lifter!" he shouted. He took the most detestable of all animals and laid it on the altar. He raised his mighty sword and sliced open his sacrifice. Blood splattered the face and hands and body of Madman. The people were shocked by this supreme act of rebellion against the one who holds stars in his hands.

But this was only the beginning. Madman forbid anyone to look beyond the sky or listen to the wind or walk the ways of Heart-Lifter. In the streets, sacred scrolls were burned. Anyone found to own or read the scrolls was put to death. Soldiers forced all to bow before Shining One. Those who hesitated were sold into slavery in the northern cities of the Kingdom of the Leopard.

Amid this desolation, many fled to the highland caverns. Among them was an Elderly Keeper and his five sons. They slipped past sleeping soldiers late one night and made their way to the hills a short day's journey to the west. They hid in the wild and lived off the land.

Troops were sent out to hunt down those who had escaped. When anyone was found, they were asked, "Shining One or death?" Those who bowed to Shining One were spared. Those who would not died. Stories multiplied of the courage of those who died speaking the name of Heart-Lifter. These stories forged iron resolve in the People of Promise.

Soldiers marched into the small mountain village of the five sons and shouted, "Shining One or death?" The Elderly Keeper stepped forward to face the soldiers.

"Do as Madman commands," said the officer. "We will honor you with gifts. All you must do is to sacrifice a detestable animal upon this altar."

"This altar belongs to Heart-Lifter. Keep your silver and gold, for we shall never deny the one beyond the sky by making such a sacrifice."

A young man who tended sheep in the nearby meadows ran forward to stand by the altar. "I will accept your gifts. Allow me to sacrifice whatever you wish upon this altar."

Intent on the young man, the soldiers were not ready for the scream of rage as the Elderly Keeper rushed forward, gripping a dagger with both of his hands. Before anyone could react, he plunged it into the heart of the young man. The officer grabbed him from behind, but the old man whirled about and buried the blade into him.

Now the crowd surged forward.

Frightened soldiers retreated.

The five sons tore down the altar.

"If any wish to walk with Heart-Lifter," shouted the Elderly Keeper, "follow us." He and his sons fled with their neighbors into the rugged backcountry.

More soldiers were sent into the highlands to kill any who would not sacrifice to Shining One. Madman was determined to destroy the People of Promise, starting with the murderous old keeper and his five sons. A cycle of the moon later, runners came to Madman with word that many people had taken refuge in a large cave. The best soldiers were sent to surround the cave. Their officer shouted in, "Come out and obey Madman. Or die."

"We shall not come out!" shouted those in the cave. "We shall not sacrifice to Shining One or deny our maker. But neither will we fight you, for this day is set aside to honor Heart-Lifter."

So the soldiers of Madman entered the great cave, slaughtering every man and woman and child. A thousand People of Promise died that day, and not one of them picked up even a stone in defense.

When Elderly Keeper heard of the slaughter, he mourned deeply, but he also knew that his enemies had made a great mistake. All now lusted for their blood. He turned to his five sons and said, "It is time to fight. Whether a day of rest or a day of labor, we shall carry our swords and fight any who serve Madman. We shall not die as our friends, and we shall not let them die for nothing."

His call spread through the Land of Promise. Men of faith came to stand against Madman and the ways of Shining One. They became a mighty army that stood for the people and the nation and Heart-Lifter. They tore down evil altars and struck down those who came to destroy them and saved the lives of the innocent.

Every morning they walked the highlands.

Every noon they listened to the wind.

Every night they looked beyond the sky.

Cycles of the moon passed. Elderly Keeper was tired. His breath grew short and his vision dim and his voice cracked. The leaders of his army gathered about him.

"Fight a good fight," he said softly. "Fight until the leopard returns to his homeland, until the People of Promise can stand before their maker without fear of death. Let my sons be your leaders. Let Hammer, my third-born, take my place."

As the sun sank below the Great Sea and the stars shone forth, Elderly Keeper pointed up. "Shine as brilliantly as the stars and never forget their promise: No matter how dark the path, he will always show the way."

The old man smiled.

He closed his eyes and let go of life.

But the smile remained.

CHAPTER 11

THE HAMMER

I will make a name for myself," said a general from the City of Caravans. "I will attack Hammer and crush his men and win the approval of Madman."

So the general gathered a strong army of those who hated the People of Promise and went out to battle. The army marched south, and when he was less than a day from the City of Palms, the spies of Hammer reported to their leader.

"Our enemy is great and powerful and well-equipped," said the spies.

"We are ready," said Hammer.

"But we are few and hungry and unprepared for battle."

"Victory does not depend on us," said Hammer. "Heart-Lifter is our sword and shield and strength. We must fight with all of our might, but he will win the battle. We need not be afraid."

They looked beyond the sky.

They pounced upon those who came against them.

They fought and pursued and pounded their enemy back.

Stories of their victory spread through the Kingdom of the Leopard. Those who hated Heart-Lifter shook in terror, while those who loved him rejoiced. Madman screamed and cursed and vowed to destroy Hammer and his brothers and all who fought with them. He gathered the finest forces of his kingdom and ordered them to be ready for battle. But when he went to the treasury to finance his plans, he discovered it was empty.

"What has happened to all of my silver and gold?"

"War is costly," said the chief guard of the treasury. "Your determination to destroy the People of Promise and erase their memory from the Blue Planet has had a price."

"I shall not let this stop me," he yelled at the chief guard. "If I need more money to maintain my mission, I shall find it."

Within a cycle of the moon, Madman split his army into two forces. Half of the troops were assigned to a noble general, who was told to protect the kingdom and destroy the People of Promise. Madman led the other half of his troops east across the Great River to what was once known as the Kingdom of the Bear. Here he went from city to city, demanding and plundering to fill his royal treasury.

Meanwhile the noble general sent one of his officers to search for and destroy Hammer. Thousands of soldiers marched south on the main trade route to a large grassy plain near the City of Warm Springs. When the local traders heard of this great army, they went to the chief officer with a proposal.

"Instead of killing these rebels," said the traders, "why don't you capture them, and then we will buy them from you as slaves?"

The traders set piles of silver and gold before the chief officer. He looked at the great wealth and nodded his approval of the trader's proposal. "Madman will be proud of my actions if I can defeat the People of Promise and at the same time fill the royal treasury."

Hammer and his men hid nearby. They watched the large army set up camp. They watched the traders make their proposal. They watched the chief officer accept it.

"They can deal all they want," said Hammer, "but we shall prevail.

"We shall unite our people

"and fight for our faith

"and cleanse our sanctuary."

All his men looked beyond the sky and asked that Heart-Lifter's hand be on them. Then they fasted and tore their clothes and read the sacred scrolls. With a trumpet blast, his men were called before him.

As dusk was turning to dark, Hammer shouted, "I only want the most faithful to fight beside me. If you are fainthearted or newly married or planting vineyards, it is time for you to return home."

Some said good-bye and left the camp. Then a few more followed their example. Soon a large portion of Hammer's men were walking away.

"Early tomorrow morning we shall fight," Hammer said to those who were left. "Our numbers are small and our enemy is great, but we shall not lay down our weapons. It is better to die in battle than live in bondage."

The men cheered and the sun set and Hammer went to his tent. But before he fell into sleep, a runner entered the camp.

"Our enemy has left his tent. He is planning to attack us in the still of night while we are deep in sleep."

"Then let us take their camp while they are away," smiled Hammer.

Swiftly and quietly, the warriors of Hammer marched through the darkness toward the tents of their enemy. But as the sun lifted above the Mountains of the Dawn, Hammer saw that there were still many men in the enemy camp.

"Even a portion of their army is too great for us," said his men.

"We need not fear," said Hammer. "For the one who holds stars in his hands shall give us victory. Let us look to the sky and crush this army."

As the trumpets broke the morning, the men of promise charged their enemy. The Army of the Leopard awoke and panicked and fled. Hammer's men pursued and won a great victory and killed many of their enemies.

Meanwhile the chief officer of the Army of the Leopard discovered that Hammer's camp was empty. He laughed and said, "Hammer is a coward. He saw us coming and has fled for the hills."

But as the chief officer turned toward his camp, he saw billows of gray smoke rising above the ridge. Moving closer, he saw that his camp was captured and his men were gone and his tents were in flames. Standing in the midst of it all with swords outstretched were Hammer and his men.

The Army of the Leopard was deeply afraid.

"The victory belongs to Heart-Lifter," shouted Hammer as he watched his enemy turn its back on the camp and flee to the hills. "And this camp belongs to us."

His men plundered everything around them. They seized all the silver and gold left by the local traders. They captured swords and shields, purple cloth and fine jewelry and great riches. Then they looked beyond the sky and thanked their maker for the day and the victory and the plunder.

The chief officer led the remains of his army north and reported what had happened to Noble General.

"So the People of Promise now hold the main trade route to the City of Palms?" asked the general.

"Yes, that is true," said the chief officer, "but we still hold the city itself and we have a strong garrison there."

"If Madman hears of this loss, our lives will be in danger."

So the next spring Noble General mustered a larger army than before. He personally marched them past the City of Palms to a field near the Valley of Apples where they met Hammer.

"They have six times as many soldiers as we have," said one of the brothers to Hammer. "They have horsemen, and we have none."

"But we have one who is infinite and eternal and all-powerful," replied Hammer. "Who else would we need?" Then he turned to the wind.

"Fill them with fear.

"Melt their boldness.

"Shake their strength.

"Let us strike them down with swords of your power and hearts that seek your smile."

Then with a mighty shout that made Noble General tremble, Hammer called his men forward. Both sides charged. But when they came crashing together, the Army of Promise fought with such valor that their enemy was shocked. Thousands of soldiers from the Kingdom of the Leopard soon lay dead on the field.

"Retreat!" shouted Noble General. "If we try to stand before these men, we shall be destroyed."

So that evening they fled north to their homeland, and Hammer turned to his brothers. "Our enemy is crushed, and the land is ours. Let us go up to the City of Palms and reclaim the sanctuary."

Hammer and his men entered their ancient city. When they approached the Special Place, tears filled their eyes.

The sanctuary was desolate.

The courtyards were overgrown.

The altar was profaned.

The People of Promise tore their clothes and cried in pain and fell face-down on the ground. Hammer sounded the trumpets and reclaimed the sanctuary. Some resisted and were quickly killed by the enraged invaders. After three long years, the Special Place was finally back in their hands. The forces of Madman had been repelled, and now his wicked stench had to be removed. The People of Promise circled the grounds, singing songs of praise and honor and commitment to the one who holds stars in his hands.

"What shall we do?" asked one of Hammer's brothers.

"We shall restore the Special Place to its glory," declared Hammer, "and we shall rededicate it to Heart-Lifter."

The people cheered and gave all they had so the sanctuary could be a place of majesty once more. Hammer chose respected men, who walked the highlands each morning with their maker, to set everything right.

During the next few cycles of the moon, much was done. The chosen men removed the statues of Shining One that Madman had placed in the sanctuary and ground the gold into dust. Every mark made by Madman was removed. The inside was purified and the outside cleansed and it all was made to shine. Candles were filled with pure oil and incense was lit, and the golden walls shimmered as in days of old.

The chosen went into the courtyard and bent their backs. Briars and brambles were uprooted. All was cleared and taken outside the city to be burned in great bonfires that brightened the night. At last the People of Promise could once again stand before the sanctuary. But stains of desecration still marked their sacred altar. Visions of Madman as he slaughtered his detestable animal made the people cringe.

The altar had to be destroyed.

Each stone was removed and carried away and buried on a lonely hillside far from the city. Unhewn stones were brought and a new altar built. When all was done, the people rejoiced and a thousand spotless, newborn lambs were sacrificed to the one above all.

"This is our day of dedication," said Hammer to the people. "The sanctuary has been reclaimed. The City of Palms has been taken. The Kingdom of Promise is free for the first time in over four hundred years."

For eight days the people celebrated.

Far to the east, Madman besieged the City of Wealth. This city was famed for its vast hoards of silver and gold. Its temple was rich, and its buildings wore an affluence that made Madman envy. He tried for many cycles of the moon to plunder this city, but strong walls and heavy gates frustrated him. So in great anger, Madman marched to the City of Stars to refresh his troops and reconsider his plans.

Royal runners came to Madman from his homeland. "Hammer and his brothers have defeated your forces two times. They have taken back their sacred sanctuary and their ancient capital and their kingdom. The People of Promise have grown very strong."

Madman held his head.

His body shook with violent tremors.

He was overcome with grief and anger and confusion.

He fell upon his bed and lay there for many days. Wild dreams haunted his nights and paranoid fears plagued his days.

"I am dying," he ranted. "I am poor and wretched and downhearted."

"No, that cannot be," said the serpent that was constantly at his side. "You are powerful and proud and beloved by all."

Madman laughed.

"You are a liar and a thief. You have led me to my fall. If I had not despised the ways of Heart-Lifter and desecrated his sanctuary and fought his people, I would not be on the edge of insanity. But here I am dying a bitter fool in a strange and lonely land."

Madman laughed again—a sad and demented laugh that sent ripples of terror through all who heard it. That night Madman died. He had seen only thirty-six summers, but he had done a lifetime of evil.

The People of Promise rejoiced, for the man who had tried to destroy them and banish their name from the Blue Planet could threaten them no more.

But their battles were not yet done.

TRULY RIGHTEOUS CAUSES
CANNOT BE OVERTHROWN
BY SCHEMES OF THE UNRIGHTEOUS.

THE BROTHERS

We must kill Hammer and his brothers," said the officers as they stood before Madman's son. "He is making the wall around the City of Palms ever stronger. If we do not attack quickly, their kingdom will never be ours."

Madman's son hated the People of Promise as much as his father had. He immediately sent a large force to level the ancient capital.

A hundred thousand soldiers.

Thirty thousand horsemen.

Thirty-two war elephants.

The brothers stood on the city wall and watched as the great army pounded on the northern gate. Hammer was the middle of the five brothers with Planner and Counselor the two older, Soldier and Persuader the two younger.

"We have never met such a force," Hammer said to his brothers. "What shall we do?"

"Lead a group of fighting men out of the city by cover of night and camp on their opposite side," said Planner. "Then they must fight on two fronts."

"Yes," said Hammer. "Tonight we shall march."

Early the next morning, Madman's son had an enemy at his back. He sounded the horns and led his men away from the city. He took his thirty-two elephants and strapped wooden carriages onto their backs. He surrounded each animal with a thousand warriors and five hundred horsemen.

As the sun rose to the roof of the sky, grapes and mulberries were crushed to enrage the elephants. The animals went wild. They snorted and trumpeted and stampeded toward Hammer's army, destroying everything in their path. The ground shook and a cloud of dust rose and the sound of such a strong force made them tremble even more.

"Forward!" shouted Hammer.

His men obeyed, in spite of overwhelming terror.

Soldier was on the front line with his sword held high. His keen eye studied the ferocious onslaught. It seemed unstoppable, but his courage did not waver as he looked for a point of weakness.

There it was, in the midst of the army. The tallest and largest of the massive elephants was covered with brightly polished armor of brass and gold that blazed in the midday sun. The carriage on its back was elegant and ornate.

"There is Madman's son," shouted Soldier to Hammer. "If he falls, his forces may lose heart."

With a mighty yell, Soldier plunged toward the royal elephant.

He fought his way to the animal until he was beneath its belly. Where the armor did not protect, he drove his sword deep into the massive beast.

The elephant reared back.

It cried out in pain.

It swayed and stumbled and collapsed.

Soldier tried to remove his sword, but by the time he pulled it free, the animal was falling. Soldier died instantly, and Madman's son leaped from the carriage and was rescued. The enemy pressed their fierce attack against Hammer without pause.

"Retreat!" shouted Hammer in shock and sadness.

His men fled to the City of Palms. Madman's son attacked the capital with siege towers and battering rams and powerful catapults. The People of Promise sent spears and arrows and fire at all who approached their walls. But after several cycles of the moon, it became clear that they could not last much longer. Supplies were running low. Food was nearly gone.

Then one afternoon, in the heat of the day, a man walked alone toward the northern gate. He had neither shield nor sword nor armor. A well-placed arrow would fell him, and archers were ready to send it.

"Stand down!" shouted the officer of the wall to his archers. "The one who approaches is Madman's son."

"We wish peace," said the unarmed man. "Let me speak with Hammer. If we can come to agreement, we shall let your city stand."

"Why do you wish peace?" asked Hammer.

"There is unrest in my palace, and my kingdom is in danger. Release all the prisoners you have captured, and we shall leave in peace."

The two leaders agreed. Early the next morning, as the sun lit the Mountains of the Dawn, the soldiers and horsemen and elephants were gone. The unrest was deep. Within a year Madman's son had been murdered by one in the royal line. This new man was a cruel king who also hated the People of Promise. He sent his general to complete the destruction of the People of Promise.

As the general stood before the City of Palms and called out to those on the walls,

"We shall crush you

"and burn your sanctuary

"and prove your maker powerless."

"The one who is infinite and eternal and all-powerful has heard your boast," called back Hammer. "He will answer."

The Army of the Leopard pushed forward with the top general leading the way. When the Army of Promise came out of the city to meet them, the general was the first to fall. The leopard fled, but Hammer pursued until many enemy warriors had fallen. The people rejoiced and celebrated and danced at the complete victory.

When Cruel King heard that his first army was no more, he sent a second, greater force, and the Army of Promise grew fearful. Many deserted their posts and hid in the hills.

Hammer looked into the eyes of those who remained and said, "You are the bravest of the brave. Let us rise up against our enemy and fight."

"We are too few to win such a battle," said Persuader.

"Then there will be honor in our courage. If we die, let us die bravely for our people."

So Hammer led his men in a valiant battle in which many fell. When the People of Promise fled the field at last, the three brothers of Hammer carried away his pierced body. Hammer was buried near a small mountain village, beside his father and mother and brother.

Disorder spread, and those who looked beyond the sky hid. But warriors who had fought under Hammer went to Persuader.

"Be our ruler and leader and king. Reclaim our kingdom."

When Cruel King heard that another of the brothers had stepped forward, he immediately sent many troops to the City of Palms to kill him. The remaining three brothers fled to the wilderness a day south of the city, near where Farmer had lived with his family.

Planner journeyed west to gather supplies. While he was there, the People of the Plains ambushed him and captured him and killed him.

Cruel King's men swarmed across the land, taking every field and valley and stream. No city was left untouched, not even the City of Palms. For seven years Persuader and Counselor lived in the wilderness. Though respected by many, they had become outlaws.

But Cruel King faced a challenge for his own throne from a grandson of Madman. To strengthen his position, he sent a letter to Persuader.

"Be my ally. I will give back the City of Palms and make you a free man."

The challenger heard of Cruel King's promise, and he too wrote a letter to Persuader.

"Be my ally. I will recognize you as king of your people and chief keeper of the sanctuary." With the letter came a heavy box containing a purple robe and a golden crown.

Cruel King sent another letter, but Persuader remembered the death of Hammer.

He remembered the years of hiding
and the oppression of his people.

He remembered, and supported the challenger.

In a few cycles of the moon, there was a new king. Persuader was invited to the royal palace, where he received honor and respect. All that had been promised was given and much more. The new king placed his arm around Persuader and announced to all his officers, "This is one of my best and treasured friends."

But several summers later, the King of Pyramids came north and attacked the new king and forced him to the desert, where nomads cut off his head.

Another challenger attempted to be king, one who had been raised on stories of Hammer's defiance of Madman. He gathered a large army to eliminate the brothers.

But when the challenger found Persuader's army, he saw that it was as large as his own. So he laid down his sword and met with Persuader. "Why have you come armed for battle?" he asked. "We come to offer peace and honor and friendship. Send your men home, for all this land belongs to you."

Persuader believed what was said. He sent many home, though he kept a thousand with him and double that near the Stormy Sea. Then he went with the new challenger into a nearby city to eat and drink and celebrate their friendship. But when they entered, the challenger's men closed the gates and turned on Persuader. They captured him and slaughtered all who were with him.

"Now we will destroy the People of Promise," shouted the challenger. "We have their leader, and their army has dispersed. Let every warrior of the surrounding peoples come together, and we will erase their name from the Blue Planet."

So a mighty army assembled. The People of Promise trembled with a fearful heart when they saw such a powerful foe.

"Have courage and stand strong!" shouted Counselor. "My brothers have fought and freed and defended this kingdom for nearly twenty years. Let it not be in vain.

"I shall lead my people

"and protect my city

"and free my brother.

"Those who surround our land shall not destroy us. Stand beside me and let us fight for victory."

The people cheered. "You are the last of the brothers. Lead us into battle and we will follow."

When the challenger heard that Counselor was ready for battle, he sent runners to the city. "We wish to do Persuader no harm. He owes us money. We are holding him until we receive what is owing. Send us a wagon of silver with his two sons, then we will release him."

"Give the challenger what he wants," insisted the people.

"He is lying," said Counselor.

"If you do not give him what he wishes, your brother's blood will be on your hands."

So Counselor sent a wagon of silver with the two sons. But the challenger did not release Persuader. He invaded the Land of Promise, but each place he attacked was passionately defended. Each time he attacked, he was blocked.

The king swore at his enemy
and killed Persuader
and departed for his homeland.

Counselor buried his brother beside his father and mother and brothers. All the people mourned for many days.

Counselor took the place of his brother, leading with courage and wisdom and integrity. He built up the strongholds with high towers and thick walls and heavy gates. He held his land and chased away its enemies. He looked beyond the sky and walked with Heart-Lifter and sacrificed spotless, newborn lambs to the maker of all.

The people tilled their land in peace.

They harvested their fields in prosperity.

They ate their fruit in abundance.

Old men stood in the streets to speak of Heart-Lifter, and young men all knew of the five brothers. The people lived free and the sanctuary was clean, and the City of Palms was known throughout the Blue Planet for its trust in the one who holds stars in his hands.

Finally their enemies once again marched against the People of Promise. Counselor was too old for the rigors of battle. His vision was dim and his stamina weak and his step slow. So he called on his two oldest sons.

"For thirty years my brothers and I fought for this kingdom. Now it is you who must go out and fight for our people. May Heart-Lifter bless you."

His sons chose twenty thousand warriors and went out to fight their enemies, while Counselor stayed in the City of Palms with his youngest son. The Army of Promise pushed back the invaders. But the oldest son was wounded, and he returned to the side of his father to recover.

One of Counselor's daughters was married to a wicked man who listened to the words of Shining One. He was proud and arrogant. He placed silver and power and position above all else. He was angry that Counselor had not included him among the nation's leaders.

"If he does not give it to you," whispered the snake, "take it. Kill the father and his sons and make the kingdom yours."

So the son-in-law gave a great banquet and surrounded the room with men. Counselor and two of his sons came, but the secondborn was out with the troops. When Counselor and his sons had drunk much wine, the son-in-law struck them down. Then he sent men to find the remaining son. But warning reached him first, and the son seized those who came for him. The next day his brother-in-law was arrested for murder, and Counselor's Son was crowned king of the Land of Promise.

As he laid his father beside his famous brothers, he spoke gently to his people.

"Five brothers looked beyond the sky.

"Five brothers fought for freedom.

"Five brothers died for this kingdom."

And the people wept.

THE FUTURE
WAS ALL GOOD.
THERE WAS PEACE.
THE LAND PROSPERED.

CHAPTER 13
THE FUTURE

The Kingdom of Promise stretched its boundaries as it had in the days of Wise King.

Every morning for thirty years Counselor's Son, king of the Land of Promise, rose before the brightness touched the Mountains of the Dawn and walked the highlands with Heart-Lifter. They talked and laughed and shared their hearts as Man and Garden-Maker had many millennia before.

One morning in the season when rains came and winter lilies bloomed, Counselor's Son felt both weary of his rule and restless of heart. He set out toward the south from the City of Palms. He walked through the morning and the warm afternoon. Soon the land was cooling with the evening breeze, but Counselor's Son felt drawn on. He smelled the sweet aroma of honeysuckle as turtledoves cooed and ravens hurried toward their nests. He sat in the tall grass and watched a fragile fawn take its first wobbly steps. Late-season apples and pomegranates and apricots hung unharvested on the wild ancient trees. Counselor's Son plucked a globe of golden fruit and bit deep into its sweet flesh.

"Is it good?" called a tanned young man who came wading through the grass. His staff and plain wool robe were those of a truth teller.

"It is very good and very special somehow," answered Counselor's Son as he wiped sticky juice from the corners of his mouth. "What is this place?"

"It is the ancient Valley of Apples."

"The valley which Promise-Keeper first brought Merchant? It is beautiful."

"Yes," said the young man. "And now Promise-Keeper is Heart-Lifter, and he has brought you here so we can talk."

"What words do you have for me?"

"You are of the Dynasty of the Brothers, but you are not of Shepherd's royal line. Therefore, you and your sons and your grandsons can never be true kings of the People of Promise."

"Who shall be the true king?"

"Many years ago, Writer told of one who would come as a great light in a dark time. This king is still to come, and he will reign as king of all kings ever born upon the Blue Planet. He will be called:

"Wonderful,

"Mighty,

"Everlasting."

"When can we expect to see such a great king?" asked Counselor's Son.

"Many summers must pass," said the truth teller. "But when a brilliant star shines over the City of Hope, the People of Promise will know that the king has been born."

"Will I live to see the birth of the king?"

"Your time on the Blue Planet has come to an end. Today you will walk beyond the sky and visit the house of the one who holds stars in his hands."

"But what shall become of the kingdom? My children do not listen to the wind or read the sacred scrolls or follow the ways of their maker."

"Have you taught them the promise of the rainbow?"

"Yes."

Suddenly clouds moved in from the Great Sea and drifted across the sky to the north and south. A warm shower fell upon the two men, but they stood still, and neither sought shelter or covered his head. With eyes wide open, they looked beyond the sky and let the water run down their faces like streams of unhindered tears.

Then they saw.

The sun pushed through and sparkled on the showering droplets, creating a brilliant rainbow that stretched in the direction of the City of Palms. Both men gasped at its beauty and whispered in awe at a truth they had known since youth: "He is always close and he will always care."

The two men talked as the rainbow faded and the sun set and the stars claimed their place. A pleasant, intriguing scent mingled with honeysuckle and encircled the conversation.

"What a wonderful smell," said Counselor's Son, "so strong and delightful and stirring."

"It is the scent of eternity," said the young man.

And then the scent was gone, and Counselor's Son's body crumpled amid the grass. Counselor's Son had journeyed on, beyond the sky. For the next forty summers, his sons and grandsons ruled the Kingdom of Promise. Then the Dynasty of the Brothers was cut short as the powerful Kingdom of the Eagle swept down upon the City of Palms. The Army of Promise fought to its death. Twelve thousand warriors bravely gave their lives in defense of the ancient capital.

The dynasty ended.

The city fell.

The kingdom was enslaved once more.

The new conquerors listened to the words of Shining One. They were people of arrogance and art who wished to leave their mark on every tribe within their extensive borders. They placed a Paranoid King over the People of Promise. This king fought his way to power and murdered any who opposed him.

Paranoid King was a man of contrasts: He was a great builder who cared nothing about preserving what was good in his nation. He could be lavishly generous and murderously ruthless. He was noble and violent, sensitive and cruel. He had ten wives, but the only one he truly loved was a descendant of Counselor's Son. Through this marriage, he acquired the illusion that he belonged on the throne and renewed the Dynasty of the Brothers. But her family did not approve of the king's conduct or character, and they scoffed at his pretension.

Paranoid King was outraged. No one dare question him, especially true heirs to a dynasty. The king killed his wife's mother and brothers. Then he killed his true love and her two sons. Above all else, he wanted to be respected and remembered and honored. He built a grand palace in the City of Palms with gold and marble. He built auditoriums and amphitheaters and monuments.

After twenty summers, Paranoid King sent a proclamation throughout the nation. "Many of you look beyond the sky and listen to the wind and sacrifice spotless, newborn lambs to Heart-Lifter. But the splendor of the Special Place has faded, and it is no longer worthy of the one who holds stars in his hands."

The people looked at the sanctuary and agreed. Time and conquerors had done much damage.

The stones had crumbled.

The timbers had rotted.

The silver and gold had been stripped away by leopard kings.

"The Special Place has seen five hundred summers, and even when it was new it was nothing like the magnificent sanctuary built by Wise King. I will restore this special place to what it should be. This will be my most noble achievement."

So Paranoid King tore apart the sacred sanctuary and excavated to bedrock. He greatly enlarged the design and laid new foundation stones. Every material was the best. He refused to look beyond the sky, but he wished to win the hearts of the People of Promise. The walls were of finely cut and polished stone covered with gleaming white marble accented by silver and gold. Multiple rows of massive white marble columns lined the Special Place, and brilliantly finished bronze doors, twelve times the height of a grown man, welcomed the keepers. This was surrounded by expansive inner and outer courtyards.

Eighteen thousand workers swarmed over the sanctuary for nine years, and the people of the city stood in breathless wonder at its inspiring splendor. Facing the Mountains of the Dawn was the Beautiful Gate, and the morning sun reflected a brilliance that dazzled all who saw it.

"The Special Place is a most lovely and elegant building," said an ancient truth teller. "But it will not win the hearts of the people."

Paranoid King heard these words and almost had the truth teller killed for his insolence. But the truth teller was venerated in the wilderness community that stood among the cliffs on the western shore of the Salty Sea. These people set themselves apart. They were a people of discipline and virtue and devotion to understanding the ancient words of promise.

They would walk with Heart-Lifter.

They would listen to the wind.

They would study the sacred scrolls.

Paranoid King summoned the ancient truth teller and asked in frustration, "Why won't I win the hearts of the people?"

"The people know you are not the true king."

"I am the true king."

"When I was a young man I spoke to Counselor's Son of this. Now I shall tell you. Do you wish to know the future?"

"Yes," said the king, though he was angry that the calm man showed neither awe nor fear nor homage in his presence.

"It is written that a young virgin will have a baby and he will be a son, and his name will be a reminder that the one above all is with us. A brilliant star will shine above the City of Hope on the night of his birth. He shall be a great king of the royal line of Shepherd.

"He shall conquer every kingdom

"and heal every hurt

"and bring peace to the Blue Planet."

"It is ridiculous to speak of peace throughout the Blue Planet," Paranoid King said in derision.

"Nothing is impossible with Heart-Lifter," said the truth teller with the gentle voice of one teaching a child. "Our king shall always look beyond the sky, and he shall be like no other man that has ever been known. He shall reject the wrong and choose the right. He shall make the blind to see and the lame to walk and the dead to rise again. He shall strip away all the power of Shining One."

"You are a crazy old man," laughed the king. "You have lived too long under the hot desert sun."

"Our future king shall be welcomed through the gates of the City of Palms with rejoicing. He will bring hope and take up our difficulties and carry our sorrows. In the end he will be crushed so that we might live."

"Crushed? He will not be such a great king then, will he?"

"He shall be rejected and bruised and broken, but his days shall never end."

"Everyone dies," said Paranoid King.

"In this king, death will learn its limits," said the old man. He smiled as one who saw glimpses of wondrous things.

"Enough of this foolishness!" shouted the king. "Out of my sight! Leave my city at once, or you shall die."

"I will go with a glad heart," said the truth teller. "But first tell me: Do you know the promise of the stars?"

"No! And I do not care!"

"When you look up into the night sky and see the stars with the greatest fire, then remember the promise of the one who holds them in his hands. The promise is that no matter how dark the path, he will always show the way."

The Paranoid King was silent.

The ancient truth teller said one more sentence before he turned his back.

"When you see the brilliant star over the City of Hope, you will find the future of the Blue Planet."

EPILOGUE

The crackling branches in the fire pit flamed merrily. Then, when too much had burned away to hold them up, they collapsed into a pile of glowing embers that put out little light.

But that was all right. The storyteller had been talking about the one who held stars in his hands, and in the darkness the people all spent long moments beholding his handiwork.

"It is finished. I have spoken all that I have held and read and copied in the ancient scrolls."

The girl child of nine summers suddenly jumped to his side with some excitement.

"Tell the secret: Who was the truth teller who spoke to Paranoid King?" she said mysteriously.

"Secrets are not for fireside circles, Granddaughter," said the old man chuckling. "But it is no secret. I was that man, though I doubt Paranoid King would wish to see my face again."

"And you said the story is finished," pressed the girl.

"Someday Heart-Lifter will finish it. But everything has been said that is in the scrolls."

"Look, Grandfather," she said, pointing up. "Not everything is written."

The old man smiled as he looked high in the western sky where she pointed. Then his smile faded and he stood. She was right. That was a brilliant star. No, . . . brighter than brilliant. Its light bore a hole through the darkness. They were only a few miles from the very City of Hope. It could not be, could it?

He rubbed his old eyes and strained to see.

Now everyone was staring.

And at last the old man gasped.

"My friends, I believe the future is upon us," he said in awe.

"Does this mean our new king is here?" whispered the girl.

"It means. . . Yes, I think that is what it means. I hope so. Though about now he may be just a wrinkled little baby, not much heavier than a newborn lamb. But he is Heart-Lifter's greatest gift."

The small circle listened silently, intently, as the old man repeated the promises of the future king. The flocks were miles off this night, even closer to the City of Hope. Everyone wondered if they too were watching the sky. And every eye remained fixed on the star.

WHO WAS THAT?
WHERE IS THAT?

Names of people and places used in these stories correspond to the names of people and places in the Bible. Names were chosen to highlight or interpret some aspect of the character and life story of the person. The same was done with the place names. Because of changes in the lives of some of the people who appear, more than one name is sometimes given. Below are the biblical names corresponding to those used by the storyteller with a hundred wrinkles.

IMPORTANT PEOPLE

Assassin King	Shallum
Bald Man	Korah
Beekeeper's Wife	Deborah
Besieged King	Jehoahaz
Book King	Josiah
Boy King	Joash
Brave King	Xerxes
Bride	Rebecca
Brother	Aaron
Builder	Noah
Castle King	Ahab
Castle Queen	Jezebel
Cedar King	Jehoahaz
Challenger King	Jeroboam
Chosen King	Rehoboam
Committed King	Hezekiah
Conquering King	Amaziah
Counselor	Simon Maccabee
Counselor's Son	John Hyrcanus
Cruel King	Demetrius I
Dark King	Baasha
Defiant King	Pekah
Desert Prince	Haman
Desperate King	Hoshea
Dreamer	Joseph
Elder Sister	Leah
Elderly Keeper	Mattathias Maccabee
Farmer	Amos
Father	Abraham
Father-in-Law	Laban
Final King	Zedekiah
Fire King	Ahaz
First Born	Cain before the murder of Abel
First King	Saul
Gatekeeper	Elimelech

Gatekeeper's Wife	Naomi
General	Moses
General King	Menahem
Generous King	Artaxerxes
Giant	Goliath
Good King	Asa
Grandfather	Methuselah
Grandson	Zerubbabel
Great Conqueror	Alexander the Great
Hammer	Judas Maccabee
Handmaiden	Hagar
Handmaiden's Son	Ishmael
Hated King	Amon
Humble King	Omri
Hunter	Nimrod
Innkeeper	Rahab
Keeper	Eli
Land Baron	Job
Landowner	Boaz
Last Bear King	Darius III
Laughter	Isaac
Left Hand	Ehud
Leper King	Azariah/Uzziah
Leper's Son	Jotham
Lightning	Barak
Lion	Othniel
Listener	Elisha
Loner	Samson
Longest King	Manasseh
Madman	Antiochus Epiphanes
Maiden Queen	Esther
Man	Adam
Merchant	Abraham
Mighty Warrior	Gideon
Nephew	Lot
Old Encourager	Haggai
Outcast	Jephthah
Outlaw	Cain after the murder of Abel
Outsider	Ruth
Paranoid King	Herod the Great
Planner	John Maccabee
Point Man	Joshua
Prince	Jonathan
Princess Mother	Sarah
Prosperous King	Jeroboam II
Proud King	Zimri
Persuader	Jonathan Maccabee
Rebel	Absalom
Red	Esau

Reluctant Prophet	Jonah
Renegade	Abimelech
Sailor King	Jehoshaphat
Schemer	Jacob
Scribe	Mordecai
Second Born	Abel
Seer	Elijah
Shepherd King	David
Shepherdess	Rachel
Shopkeeper	Hosea
Short King	Elah
Sister	Miriam
Sky	Daniel
Soldier	Eleazar Maccabee
Sorcerer	Balaam
Speaker	Samuel
Star	Esther
Strong King	Jehoash
Sword King	Jehu
Third Born	Seth
Tribute King	Jehoiakim
Trusted Keeper	Jehoiada
Uncrowned King	Zerubbabel
Walker	Enoch
Wall Builder	Nehemiah
Warrior King	Abijah
Watchman	Ezekiel
Weeping Prophet	Jeremiah
Wicked Queen	Athaliah
Winter King	Jehoiachin
Wise King	Solomon
Woman	Eve
Wrestler	Jacob
Writer	Isaiah
Young Encourager	Zechariah

IMPORTANT PLACES

City of Blood	Nineveh
City of Books	Debir
City of Caravans	Damascus
City of Crossroads	Haran
City of Death	Ai
City of Harvest	Jezreel
City of Hope	Bethlehem
City of Lime	Sodom
City of Lions	Dan
City of Oaks	Shechem
City of Palms	Jerusalem
City of Priests	Nod

City of Refuge	Ramoth-Gilead
City of Safety	Jabesh-Gilead
City of Springs	Rabbah (Amon)
City of Stars	Babylon (city)
City of Sight	Dotham
City of the Moon	Ur
City of the Ridge	Gibbethon
City of the Stream	Aphek
City of the Sun	Heliopolis
City of the Tower	Mizpah
City of Warm Springs	Emmaus
City of Wealth	Acco (Ptolemais)
City on the Hill	Gibeon, Samaria
Coral Sea	Persian Gulf
Double City	Hazor
Falling River	Jabbock Brook
Fortress City	Jericho
Garden	Eden
Golden River	Tigris River
Great River	Euphrates River
Great Sea	Mediterranean Sea
Green Mountain	Mount Caramel
Harbor Town	Ezion-Geber
Kingdom of the Bear	Persian Empire
Kingdom of the Bull	Assyrian Empire
Kingdom of the Dragon	Babylonian Empire
Kingdom of the Eagle	Roman Empire
Kingdom of the Leopard	Macedonian/Greek Empire
Kingdom of the Pyramids	Egypt
Land of Deltas	Egypt
Land of Promise	Israel
Lofty City	Ramah
Place of Peace	Shiloh
Place of the Portal	Bethel
Protected City	Susa
Rippling Spring	Spring of Harod
Roundtop Mountain	Mount Tabor
Royal City	Samaria (capital of the Northern Kingdom)
Royal City of First King	Gibeah
Salty Sea	Dead Sea
Stormy Sea	Sea of Galilee
Tropical Ocean	Indian Ocean
Valley of Apples	Hebron
Valley of Flames	Valley of Hinnom
Valley of Harvest	Plain of Jezreel
Western River	Kishon River
Wide River	Nile River
Winding River	Jordan River